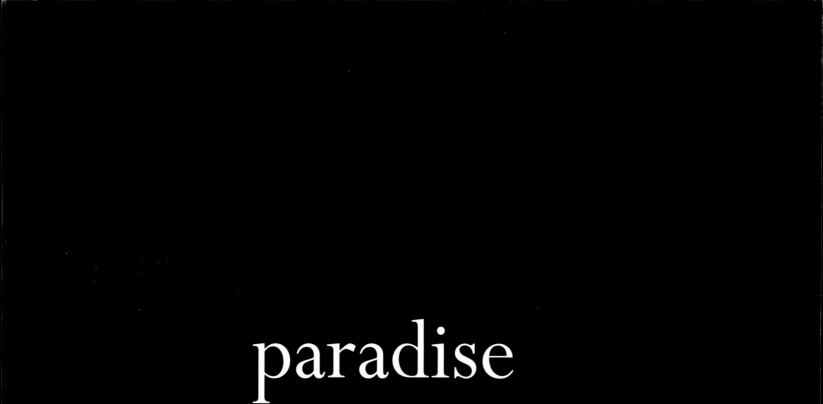

paradise

found

Photographs by Melba Levick

Text by Stanley Young

paradise found

the beautiful retreats

and sanctuaries

of california and the southwest

CHRONICLE BOOKS
San Francisco

Printed in Hong Kong.

Book and cover design by ADELAIDA MEJIA DESIGN, SAN FRANCISCO

Library of Congress Cataloging-in-Publication Data :

Levick, Melba.

Paradise Found : The Beautiful Retreats and

Sanctuaries of California and the Southwest

photographs by Melba Levick: text by Stanley Young

p. cm.

ISBN 0-8118-0687-1

1. Retreats—California Directories. 2. Retreats—Southwest. New—Directories.

3. Monasteries—California—Guest accomadations—Directories.

4. Monasteries—Southwest, New—Guest accomadations—Directories.

I. Young, Stanley, 1948– . II. Title.

BL2525.L48 1995

94-12339

CIP

291.6'5'02579—dc20

Distributed in Canada by Raincoast Books,

8680 Cambie Street, Vancouver, B.C. V6P 6M9

10 9 8 7 6 5 4 3 2 1

Chronicle Books

275 Fifth St.

San Francisco, CA 94103

COLORADO

Denver •

Benet Pines Retreat Center

Nada Hermitage

ARIZONA

Healing Center of Arizona

Arcosanti

• Phoenix

Tucson •

Picture Rocks Retreat /
Desert House of Prayer

Lama Foundation
Ghost Ranch Conference Center
Monastery of Christ in the Desert

Santa Fe   • Pecos Benedictine Monastery

NEW MEXICO

CALIFORNIA

Shenoa Retreat & Learning Center

Wellspring Renewal Center

Harbin Hot Springs

Westerbeke Ranch
Conference Center

Silver Penny Farm

Green Gulch Farm Zen Center

• San Francisco

Tassajara Zen Mountain Center

Esalen Institute

New Camaldoli Hermitage

Santa Barbara
• Mount Calvary Retreat House
Immaculate Heart / La Casa de Maria
Ojai Foundation
Serra Retreat   Saint Andrew's Abbey
• Los Angeles

contents

I dedicate this book to all the gentle souls who so graciously opened the doors

of their communities and shared their food, their thoughts, and their hearts with me; to Melba,

for her lively suggestions and friendship; and to Janice and Alyssa, for their constant love and support.

—Stanley Young

There comes a time when each of us needs to just sit quietly, rest, reassess, and breathe deeply. All the destinations described in this book provide the structure, the setting, and the support to do just that. Each in its own unique fashion is an oasis of calm, an environment whose sole purpose is to provide the time, the space, the silence, and the solitude to refresh the mind, renew the spirit, and heal the body.

For solitude sometimes
is best society
And short retirement
urges sweet return.
—Milton, *Paradise Lost*

Who would benefit from a stay at one of these sanctuaries and retreats? Anyone. Harried professionals and overworked caregivers. Mechanics. Couples seeking to reappraise their relationship. Individuals whose lives are in transition. Individuals who want their lives to be in transition. Executives. Those surviving a midlife crisis. Those enjoying late-life freedom. Gardeners and psychiatrists. Those recovering from illnesses, breakups, or addiction. Individuals seeking to connect, or reconnect, with nature, with God. Bus drivers. Individuals searching for their inner self, their inner voice, or their inner child. Artists. Roofers. Scientists. Homemakers. You. Each of these sanctuaries and retreat centers welcomes seekers of peace and insight from every walk of life and of every denomination.

These spiritual communities are not, for the most part, getaways, and although most of them are affordable, it would be an act of bad faith to treat them as simply handy and inexpensive places to stay. The object of a visit to one of these destinations is an inward exploration, and if at least a portion of your agenda does not include a large measure of searching for solitude, peace, and inner renewal, you may be better off choosing a more conventional vacation spot.

All these centers are deeply relaxing environments, and many of the sanctuaries invite the visitor to get in touch with regions of the heart, the self, and the soul that have been neglected and hidden by the endless rush of daily life. The degree of involvement is entirely up to each visitor. Time spent at these sanctuaries may be merely peaceful and calming, or it can involve a demanding quest, a thoroughgoing reappraisal of one's life, requiring a total sense of engagement and, often, a courageous opening of the heart.

In return for an innermost effort, the visitor to a sanctuary can be assured that his or her quest for inner peace will be supported and nurtured with respect. That support is a constant at each destination: If

or when you need guidance, someone to listen attentively to your concerns or share your joys and your sorrows, there is someone there. But be forewarned: These are retreat centers, temples, monasteries, and communities. They are not hospitals or clinics with care facilities. The staff members are not equipped to deal with major psychological crises. Don't arrive expecting to be cured; arrive expecting, through the silence and rhythms of each community, to discover how to allow the healing process to begin.

These sanctuaries and retreats share so much—sanctity and peace, a focus on community, a respect for worship, solitude, and contemplation—but they are as different from one another as the terrains they cover and the panoramas they overlook.

Their settings vary from the old-growth forests and misty recesses of the Pacific coast to the sunbaked canyons in northern New Mexico. Some are an easy drive off of major highways and close to large cities. Others are remote and isolated, requiring an hour's careful drive down a dusty mountain road. No matter what the physical setting, each sanctuary and each community displays deep reverence for the sacred quality of the land

it occupies and for the myriad forms of life its portion of the planet supports. A visit to a sanctuary is always a chance to get in touch with the earth and share a profound sense of place.

The number of guests varies widely. At some centers, there may be only a handful; at others, hundreds of guests may swirl around you. But community is a constant element in each sanctuary, whose usual population may range from a few dedicated individuals at one retreat to a resident community of well over a hundred at another.

Whatever its size or composition, visiting these centers means being invited to share the spiritual practices and rhythms of each community. Some of these rhythms and practices may be austere or rigorous, requiring respectful silence, prayer, or meditation. Elsewhere—and sometimes at the same center!—there may be exuberant dancing, childlike play, singing, and drumming. There are, indeed, many ways to worship and celebrate.

A visit to a sanctuary may include study and learning. Several retreat centers offer weekend workshops on a bewildering array of subjects, both religious and secular. At these gatherings, visitors can discover—and experience—everything from naturopathic healing methods and massage techniques to still-life photography and contemplative prayer.

The cuisine is easily as diverse as the styles of celebration. Meals at these centers are always healthful and prepared with a great deal of love, but the food can range from the prosaic to the positively ethereal. At some retreats, gourmet fare is exquisitely prepared, meticulously presented, and elegantly served at lamp-lit tables. At others, somewhat indifferent cafeteria staples may be served on plastic dishes and eaten at formica-covered tables under fluorescent lighting.

The accompanying styles of grace differ among communities, too. At some retreats, song and prayer may precede a meal; at others, a moment of silence and a grateful joining of hands is all the ceremony that is required. Accommodations are, by and large, clean and very basic, in keeping with a prevailing desire to pare down to essentials. However, even in this there is great diversity. Visitors may spend the night in a handcrafted bed in a baronial mansion filled with priceless antiques—or on a sleeping pad in an unadorned dormitory. No matter. The fresh air, the healthful food, and the pervasive silence will ensure a good night's sleep. Group facilities vary, too. There may be comfortable meeting rooms, strikingly designed chapels, and airy dining rooms—or groups may meet around a fire, worship in a modest structure, and eat outside.

Forms of worship vary, too. In some centers, prayer is vocal and performed

several times a day, with established rituals, music, and chants of haunting beauty. In others, worship is a more personal and informal undertaking. Given the striking natural settings, simply taking the time to examine a newly blossomed flower, admiring the stark vista of a wind-hewn mountain, or standing in the shade of a five-hundred-year-old redwood becomes a form of worship, an instant of communion, a healing moment.

After a while, those moments of peace and communion, supported by the warmth of the community, blend into the silence and beauty of the setting. The separate pieces of the self fall into place. A calming peace touches the heart of the harried visitor and bestows upon him or her a sense of tranquillity and delight, opening a door into paradise.

That is the gift-power these sanctuaries share, despite their many differences: the ability to embrace and touch each visitor in individual and inexplicable ways. Some visitors regain a sense of sheer delight, simplicity, and wonder not felt since childhood. Others may experience a sense of peace that, as the poets put it, "surpasseth understanding."

Time slows. Nights feel colder and the skies turn impossibly star laden. The noonday sun seems hotter and brighter. The outlines of leaves and mountains turn sharp. The grace and power of the sanctuary melt away the feelings of stress, leaving in their place an overwhelming sense of freedom, a joyful well-being, and an indelible appreciation of the sanctity of life.

These experiences can be life altering, but not every visit to one of the sanctuaries needs to be so overwhelmingly transformative. Many visitors return to a favorite sanctuary each year for a spiritual and mental tune-up, with no groundbreaking insights or revelations. Still, even a few days' profound relaxation and rejuvenation is a small miracle in these hurried times.

Because the affiliations of the sanctuaries are so diverse, it is highly recommended—and often required—that you contact a sanctuary before your visit, even if you are only planning a day trip. (Many communities have weeks or days of silence and seclusion.) Ask for the center's literature and know what is expected of visitors before you arrive; there are often specific rules and practices concerning comportment and behavior.

For those of you who have never spent any time at a sanctuary or a retreat, try visiting one for a day or a weekend. Many of the places in this book offer introductory workshops and courses. These are excellent for newcomers, allowing them to taste the offerings at a particular setting in the company of like-minded people. The structure of the group gathering makes it easier to get used to the rhythms of the center or community, and there is always ample free time to enjoy the setting and the people who live there. Once you have experienced the nature of a specific sanctuary in a group setting, you may then choose to return there on your own for an extended stay.

Paradise Found is only a brief introduction to the world of the spiritual retreat: a picture window revealing these special places. What is outside that window frame is for you to discover: the smell of chaparral, the aroma of incense, the sound of bells and chimes, the distant echoes of chanting or prayer carried upon a gentle evening breeze.

Consider each brief chapter covering a sanctuary as an invitation. Then accept the invitation to investigate and explore on your own. Discover the power and the magic of these extraordinary environments, and allow these remarkable communities to touch your life through the presence of the beautiful, the ineffable, and the extraordinary.

The name *Shenoa* comes from a Native American word that means "the serenity and peace you find in nature." The name for this community is apt. For ten thousand years, the Pomo Indians lived in these woods, spending their summers by the cool mountain brooks. Some say their spirit still pervades the land.

Today, Shenoa is a popular retreat center, and its guests continue to enjoy the natural beauty of the green and primeval forest in an area where Douglas firs and mammoth redwoods, hundreds of years old, stand untouched by the axe or chainsaw.

Even a short stay in these woods is enough to reveal its many faces. When the fog hangs in the trees in spring and winter, the forest falls silent, cloaked in a mysterious quiet. On even the hottest days of summer, the canopy high overhead provides shade before the breezes rush in from the ocean twenty miles away, rustling the leaves and cooling the forest.

Shenoa Retreat and Learning Center

P.O. Box 43

Philo, California 95466

707/895-3156

Shenoa was first developed as a rustic getaway called "The Pines" in the 1900s. Following World War II, more structures were added and it was renamed El Rancho Navarro, after the river that carves out the eastern perimeter of these 160 acres. During the 1950s, it was a children's summer camp, and in 1987, the property was acquired by

A vision without a task is but a
dream.
A task without a vision is
drudgery.
A vision and a task is the hope
of the world.
—Inscription in a church in
Essex, England

former members of Findhorn, a community in Scotland that pioneered a spiritual approach to the earth, growing food, and communal life.

While the original inspiration behind Shenoa was Findhorn, it is no clone of that community. "It's our ancestral connection," quips one community member. One definite Findhorn connection is found in the one-acre herb, vegetable, and flower garden by the meadow. It is sustainable, completely organic, and, as one would discover at Findhorn, laid out in the shape of a mandala. The innovative technique of alternating banks of flowers and vegetables is said to help pest management, but whatever its purpose, the result in summer is a vegetable patch that is also a riot of color and a paradise of floral and herbal scents; as healing as it is productive. Produce that goes unused is taken by guests and donated to homeless shelters in the Bay Area.

The shared focus on stewarding the land and all that grows on it is another link Shenoa shares with Findhorn. The members of this community care deeply for the land, believing that it is crucially necessary that all the residents, the guests, and future generations be able to experience the healing quality of nature in a setting that nourishes both body and spirit.

Beyond this central respect for the earth, opinions and beliefs at Shenoa vary widely. "In entering Shenoa," says one staff member, "I realized I had come to a place that was the integration of people from many tribes." Achieving consensus among the disparate opinions at Shenoa while also supporting the individual goals of other members is an achievement that the community feels will ultimately have reverberations well beyond these wooded acres. "If we can create a harmonious environment within our own diversity," says one member, "it's a step to making a harmonious environment in the world." Striving for harmony is a hallmark of this community and creates a pervasive spirit of caring at Shenoa. "It's a nurturing staff," says one member, "and a nurturing piece of land."

The rustic cabins, once part of a rustic summer camp, are surrounded by Douglas fir. Walks through Shenoa's grounds lead to secluded groves and silent meadows.

During late spring and early summer, Shenoa is booked with a wide selection of retreat groups. There is a Deep Ecology Summer Institute, several Elderhostels, yoga weekends, a women's retreat, Voice Dialogue training, and a series of alternative energy seminars.

Besides the forest setting, guests at Shenoa are treated to some fine cooking, too. The cooks at Shenoa delight in preparing healthful and delicious vegetarian cuisine—special diet requirements can also be accommodated on occasion—and much of the produce is homegrown. The large central lodge, all wood and stone, can serve up to one hundred guests and is the central meeting place where guests and community take meals together and eat at large family-style tables. At night, the natural stone fireplace is invariably filled with an inviting fire and surrounded by guests and residents quietly sharing thoughts over a cup of coffee or herb tea. A smaller meeting hall holds twenty-five, and another, holding up to seventy, is an ideal space for yoga, meditation, and workshops.

Accommodations for forty-four are in seventeen rustic cabins, each with its own bathroom and hot water. Several of the cabins have been renovated to accommodate families or couples. The shady camping ground has shared bathroom and shower facilities and provides additional space for between forty and fifty guests. Daily rates in the cabins, which include three meals, are moderate. Camping, at half the cabin rate, is an economical alternative. Modern, fully equipped cottages, sponsored by land stewards who live in them only part-time, can accommodate entire families and are available year-round at reasonable rates.

Individual guests are welcome at Shenoa throughout the year, but summers tend to be heavily booked with groups. A greater range of choice is available during the shoulder seasons of spring and fall. For those interested in living at Shenoa, volunteers can stay during the summers in work-exchange programs.

There are miles of hiking trails in the nearby Hendy Woods State Park, but the visitor to Shenoa does not have to go far afield to feel secluded in a wilderness setting. A short walk from the main lodge leads down to Rancheria Creek, where a cold mountain stream makes a sharp turn and riffles softly over its bed of pebbles and river rocks. The banks are covered with oak, sumac, redwood, and big-leaf maple trees, creating a forested ravine that at once inspires exploration and serenity.

top: The central lodge is a meeting place for food and conversation. Chats by the stone fireplace often linger late into the cool mountain evenings.

bottom: Built in the 1920s, this shaky bridge was used to cross the Navarro river during the winter, when water levels covered the ford below. Today, cars can reach Shenoa from a back entrance, but the bridge remains a challenging attraction.

"The attitude of the center is in the name," says Wellspring's director. For those seeking a getaway from the cares of the city, that attitude translates into a homey atmosphere that puts the brakes on the most hurried lifestyle, and an environment that gently guides the visitor into an appreciation of the simpler things in life.

Located in the Anderson Valley of Mendocino County, Wellspring was formerly Ray's Resort, a collection of small cabins and a main farmhouse built in the 1920s on the banks of the Navarro River. Families would trundle down Ray's Road in their Model-Ts to spend a week or two in the woods. Many of the original structures still remain—the trademark water tower is the most obvious—and add a definite pre-modern charm to the ambience. After Todd and Marge Evans purchased the land in 1980 and founded Wellspring, many new buildings were added. But the center retains the feeling of a lost age: a time of shaded porches, creaking garden gates, and swimming holes filled with laughing children.

The fifty-acre setting at Wellspring is rustic and pastoral. Towering maples and oaks shade the older riverside cabins. Behind them, fir and redwoods rise up to carpet the surrounding hills. The comfortable main building that doubles as a meeting place is a former

Wellspring Renewal Center

P.O. Box 332

Philo, California 95466

707/895-3893

wellspring renewal center

How wonderful it is to do
nothing—and then to rest
for an hour.
—Calligraphy found hanging
on a plum tree.

farmhouse. There is a large organic vegetable and herb garden, and an apple orchard that bears a bounteous and sweet harvest. Wild berries grow in profusion during the summer. In the spring, the broad sunny meadow that doubles as a camping ground is covered with lush grass and wildflowers.

The center's land is bordered on the west by Hendy Woods State Park, a resource that offers miles of hiking trails through some of the last old-growth redwoods in Mendocino County. A steep path down the riverbank leads to the river, where visitors enjoy a broad stony beach and reputedly the best swimming hole in the Valley. A dip in the cold river water has surely always been a welcome pastime. No doubt Pomo Indians, who once lived in the Anderson Valley, enjoyed this spot.

The water tower, no longer in use, has become the trademark of Wellspring.

The weather in the Anderson Valley is moody. Scorching days end in downright chilly evenings. Clouds borne by the afternoon breezes may fill the tree-covered valleys like an image from a Japanese woodcut. Occasionally, sudden showers may reveal double rainbows, arcing over the valley in colors of startling intensity.

Wellspring serves the Christian community of the northern Californian counties but it is also a retreat and renewal center with a decidedly ecumenical and interfaith outlook. All groups, individuals, and families who share the desire to connect with the earth, embrace the sacred, search for truth, or explore creativity are welcome. Wellspring also hosts yoga and meditation workshops, healing arts seminars, and weekend gatherings for artists, folk musicians, and storytellers. Other groups often book Wellspring, too: A harp conference was held here, a children's chorus once came to practice, and Native Americans visit occasionally to hold sweat lodge ceremonies and stay in the center's tepee. "Wellspring is about spirituality," says one staff member, "which everyone can participate in."

Indoor accommodations at Wellspring are available for fifty-five people. The small rustic cabins, with names such as Sorrell and Live Oak, are clean and simple, heated by wood burning stoves. Three housekeeping cabins are suitable for families, and two insulated lodges, Manitou and Blackberry, hold up to twenty-seven people, and have sitting rooms and modern kitchenettes. The campground holds up to an additional fifty people. Prices for both indoor lodging and camping are extremely affordable.

Three meals a day of delicious vegetarian cuisine are provided for groups of ten or more. Much of the food comes from the land itself. During the summer and early fall Wellspring, like the rest of the Anderson Valley, is renowned for its berry desserts and apple pies.

Guests help out with meal preparation and cleanup, clean up their own cabins, and are expected to donate an 'energy gift' of one hour each weekend to help with the upkeep of the grounds: gardening, clearing paths, chopping wood, and the like. "We're a community," says the director. "Everyone joins in." The result at Wellspring is a feeling of sharing and bonding in a special place that draws individuals, families, and groups back year after year. "When they're here, they don't feel like a guest," says the director. "They feel like they've come home."

Many of the buildings, such as the rustic riverside cottages set amid maples and oaks, hearken back to the time when Wellspring was a family resort. A small wood-burning stove provides heat during chilly nights, and modern skylights fill the cabins with light.

For hundreds of years, the Lake Miwok Indians held this valley in the Mayacamas Mountains sacred. Those who visit and live at Harbin today continue to feel that there is indeed something healing about this narrow upland valley and the springs that gush from the earth after their long subterranean voyages.

For visitors, the focal point at Harbin is the springs. At the popular warm pool (95 to 98 degrees Fahrenheit), talk is kept to a whisper. On new and full moons, up to a hundred people come into its healing waters for a playful celebration of song and chanting. All the pool areas are clothing optional, but everyone, no matter what their choice of dress, is made to feel welcome.

The hot pool (113 degrees Fahrenheit) is a strictly silent area and demands a form of submission to its searing heat. The adjacent spring-fed cold "plunge" afterward is galvanic, at once both shocking and invigorating. A separate shallow warm pool serves small children. The refreshing spring-fed swimming pool is bracketed by two large sunbathing redwood decks perched over the fragrant chaparral, affording a panoramic view of the valley and the silhouette of Mount Harbin to the east.

But there is a great deal more to Harbin than the acclaimed hot springs. Forty-eight rooms in Victorian-era wooden buildings have

Harbin Hot Springs

P.O. Box 782

Middletown, California 95461

707/987-2477

Like water, we are truest to our

nature in repose.

—Cyril Connolly

been tastefully refurbished and can house ninety-six people. Small dormitories handle about a dozen more, and ample camping areas along Harbin Creek and in the nearby meadow can accommodate hundreds of other visitors. The cost of the rooms, which is moderately expensive, does not include meals. Camping is an option for those on a limited budget.

Four separate workshop, conference, and retreat facilities are available. The Meadow Building, a light, airy wooden structure near the area where the Lake Miwok Indians had their fall encampment, is designed for smaller workshops of up to a hundred people. Here, folk dance classes one weekend may be followed by an intensive massage seminar the next. The solid and functional wooden Conference Center, across the creek from the main facilities, is a completely self-contained meeting hall with its own kitchen and all amenities, capable of handling 350 people.

previous page: The warm pool, just reaching body temperature, is a place to make new friends and catch up on news with old ones.

left: Many private homes of longtime community members, such as this one, are found throughout the Harbin grounds.

There is a well-run restaurant, a computerized office, a well-stocked bookstore, and sundry other buildings and dwellings, from tepees to cabins (many of them members' private residences) scattered throughout the property.

Harbin today is a thriving village and a far cry from the dilapidated remains of the turn-of-the-century Harbin Hot Springs Health and Pleasure Resort that Bob Hartley purchased in 1972 for $180,000. Hartley, a Harvard graduate and wealthy real estate entrepreneur, had the dream of transforming the long-neglected site into the home for a spiritual and therapeutic community. The first years at Harbin were a struggle, and in 1975, Hartley, who later studied kundalini

yoga and took the name Ishvara, gave Harbin to Heart Consciousness Church, the nonprofit corporation established to run the facilities, which has since paid off the mortgage. Ishvara/Hartley remains the church's president and minister.

There are no employees at Harbin. All the work and upkeep is performed by the residents, an ever-changing community of some 150 residents, of whom only about a hundred live at Harbin at any one time. The members of this community, whose ages range from twenty to fifty-five, share a constellation of beliefs, and personal empowerment and elements of the human potential movement blend into an accepting spiritual outlook that includes a respect for the earth and the environment.

Members are free to pursue their own spiritual practices, and many paths to happiness and peace coexist within the sprawling hills at Harbin. "Promoting personal transformation and spiritual well-being…is what community life at Harbin Springs is all about," writes one longtime resident.

For some, the community at Harbin also becomes a surrogate family, and many of the residents and guests stay at Harbin to be healed, physically and spiritually. "At Harbin," explained one member, "we are parenting ourselves and each other, with love for a change."

One place to meet residents is the popular Fern Kitchen, overlooking the warm pool. No meat, poultry, or fish is allowed, but otherwise, visitors and residents share the facilities. The Stonefront Restaurant, another popular location, serves breakfast and simple vegetarian fare prepared to suit most palates.

Residents are encouraged to develop personal profit-making enterprises, so there is no lack of services available, including a natural health food store and the Enlightenment Cafe by the pool. Many community members work as masseurs and offer sessions in a variety of techniques, including *watsu*, an innovative form of floating water massage developed in the warm pool at Harbin.

top: A mythical dragon, made by a frequent visitor to the hot springs, guards the entrance by Harbin's main office.

bottom: The main swimming pool, fed by natural spring waters, is surrounded by sunbathing decks.

Massage training is the theme of many of the smaller workshops held regularly at Harbin. Other weekend seminars include programs as diverse as "Healing the Father Wound," and "Wild Woman as Lover."

Yet, beyond this welter of choices and activities (not to mention the ever present lure of the baths), there is always the land itself, 1,160 acres of rugged mountainside. Paths and trails lead to all corners of the property, among them a vigorous outing to a distant "power point" followed by an easy ten-minute stroll to the simple wooden Tea House with its commanding view of the valley below.

More than just a spa or retreat center, Harbin Hot Springs is at once a visionary and down-to-earth community, a functioning example of an alternative society founded in a captivating setting and living on its own terms. "We're a rebellious bunch," explained one member, "with a commitment to love and freedom." Harbin fits well into the great tradition of visionary communities founded by pioneers and settlers who discovered the freedom they sought in the untrammeled expanses of the American West.

right: Harbin's carefully renovated main guest houses give visitors a feeling of turn-of-the-century charm. Inside, the rooms continue the Victorian theme with wicker furniture and brass beds.

bottom: The Stonefront Restaurant offers food, company, and occasionally, an evening's live entertainment.

What began as a family getaway sixty years ago in Sonoma's Valley of the Moon is today a friendly retreat center serving groups as divergent as Tibetan lamas and NASA scientists. Individuals, couples, and families are also welcome to spend needed quiet time amid the lush garden paths, the four-hundred-year-old oaks, and 150 acres of woodland and gentle hills that was once a Native American healing ground.

The ranch was purchased in 1935 by Dick Van Hoosear, an energetic hay and grain salesman, and his wife, Muriel. Working weekends, Van Hoosear transformed the land by building five rustic cottages, each of which now holds eight people.

The central lodge building, also Van Hoosear's handiwork, is made from adobe bricks, and the selection of rustic redwood slab tables and Mission-style furniture conveys a strong sense of the early hacienda era of California. Also Californian are the eclectic and delightful touches of whimsy throughout, such as the oil drum lampshades in the lodge and the small Inca heads embedded in the natural stone fireplace. Tasteful artifacts from Haiti, Mexico, and South America adorn the main lodge and each cabin. These artistic touches dispel any sense of being in an impersonal environment. Guests are made to feel that they are visitors in somebody's home.

Westerbeke Ranch Conference Center

2300 Grove Street

Sonoma, California 95476

707/996-7546

Do your best

Leave the rest

Angels do no more.

—Inscription over the door of the

kitchen

In 1977, Van Hoosear's daughter Patricia Westerbeke and her husband, Don, began operating the site as a full-fledged business. Today, Wendy, their daughter, is now Westerbeke's executive director and ensures that the family feeling she so fondly remembers from her youth will never leave the ranch.

The feeling of warm and familial hospitality is enhanced by the acclaimed cuisine at Westerbeke—the dinner bell is perhaps the most anticipated sound at the ranch. Meals are friendly get-togethers on an outdoor patio and have a Mediterranean feel. Their own garden provides many of the fresh ingredients used to prepare the vegetarian and nonvegetarian dishes cooked from recipes developed by the former longtime chef at Westerbeke, Carol Cleveland Bojarsky.

Bojarsky, a graduate of the Cordon Bleu de Paris, instilled in the kitchen the philosophy that eating should be "about joy, fantasy, creativity, love, giving, and receiving." Favorite ranch dishes include such delicacies as Mexican grilled chicken with lime marinade, curried squash and mushroom soup, tomato pesto tarts, and desserts such as mixed berry cobbler and a variety of fresh fruit sorbets. The ranch's official cookbook, with good reason, is called *A Plate of Grace*.

But there is more to Westerbeke than gastronomical delights. The setting, on the edge of the acclaimed Sonoma-Napa wine district in the gentle foothills of the Sonoma Mountains, is classic inland California. The views in all directions are soft and rolling. In spring, the land is resplendent in a hundred shades of green beneath glowering skies. In late summer, the fields in the valley turn amber and ocher, and the low profile of the Mayacamas to the west shimmers in the heat. Yet even in the driest seasons and hottest of years, Westerbeke, with its own natural spring remains a verdant oasis.

The ranch's own wooded creek canyon covers ninety acres and provides the setting for an optional Ropes course, an adventure-based curriculum using physical challenges to instill trust and teamwork. Besides the many trails and hikes available on the ranch's land, there is also a full range of activities at many nearby locations. Horses are available at nearby ranches and stables, and the thousand-acre Jack London State Park and the scenic town of Sonoma are only five minutes away by car. The Sonoma Coast State Beaches are a quick half-hour drive to the west.

Many visitors prefer to stay put on this ranch in miniature where, for a few days, Westerbeke becomes their world apart—a self-contained setting for solitude or socializing. There are several meeting halls—Westerbeke can handle a hundred guests who come for only one day—but groups of fifty-two constitute the upper limit for overnight lodging. Many of the visitors are individuals, couples, or families seeking a few days of quiet and serenity. Other guests may be groups of professional therapists, women writers, men studying shamanism, or business executives who discover that the unique setting and the shared accommodations imbue their time here with a heightened sense of communication that helps nurture ideas and creativity. Many also discover that in this intimate and green world, they also develop friendships that last a lifetime.

previous page: The rustic redwood cabins are known by the color of their trim. The ivy-colored Green Cabin blends in with purple irises. The Red Cabin overlooks the grounds surrounded by carefully tended periwinkle. Each cabin has its own distinct personality.

left: The cabins' color themes continue inside, often with folk art flourishes.

top: The shared accommodations at Westerbeke encourage shared communication.

bottom: A former Native American healing ground, Westerbeke has its own spring, which supplies the swimming pool and keeps the vegetation lush year-round.

The central lodge at Westerbeke, built by hand from adobe bricks, is its heart. A warm fire in the stone fireplace beckons in a setting that invites relaxing conversation.

The feeling of an earlier age: Hacienda-style eating in Mission-style wood and leather furniture beneath the tile overhang.

St. Francis surrounded by an assembly of California poppies.

Flowers and sunlight in an intimate setting for food and conversation.

When William Randolph Hearst II gave this seventeen-acre family
heirloom to the San Francisco archdiocese in 1986, he stipulated that the
name of their beloved country home, Silver Penny, never change. The
name derives from *Silver Pennies,* the title of a beloved collection of wist-
ful poetry for children published in the 1920s that was a favorite of the
Hearst family.

Today, this former farm tucked away in a quiet Sonoma County
hillside is open to everyone who needs renewal, retreat, and recre-
ation. "It is a place where one can stand still and pause from the
rushing through life," says one of the two staff members who live
on the site.

The farm was first settled in 1840, and the original house from that
time still stands on neighboring property. Silver Penny's main house
was built in 1899 and has since been enlarged and modernized
inside, but its turn-of-the-century charm still remains. Two large
rooms, each with a fireplace, are available for dining, meetings, or
for conducting worship services. Eight bedrooms, with names like

Silver Penny Farm

5215 Old Lakeville Road #1

Petaluma, California 94954

707/762-1498

silver penny farm

With a heaven full of stars over

my head

White and topaz and misty red

I know that I am honored to be

Witness of such majesty.

—Sara Teasdale, *Silver Pennies*

Moon Song and Quiet Eyes—titles of poems from *Silver Pennies*—can accommodate up to sixteen guests for private group retreats in modern comfort.

Outside, there is a three-bedroom and a one-bedroom cottage, both with cooking facilities. These low, simple structures are suitable for individuals, couples, or small groups. The only other building providing accommodation is also the most unusual: the water tower. A narrow staircase leads to two small wooden-clad rooms, Mrs. Hearst's former painting studio. Space in the tower is at a premium—imagine berths below decks on a small yacht—but the rooms are full of light, and the views beyond the liquid amber trees more than compensate for the limited conditions.

Gently rolling hills extend in all directions, broken only by the occasional line of eucalyptus or grove of live oaks. To the east, the southernmost foothills of the Sonoma Mountains disappear into the approaches to San Pablo Bay. To the southwest, the Petaluma River flows slowly past Cloudy Bend, and a dozen miles away, Burdell Mountain rises almost 1,500 feet from the low river valley.

While there are programmed retreats throughout the year, especially on weekends, Silver Penny is small and intimate enough during the week to provide the perfect setting for individual and unstructured retreats. Groups staying in the big house do their own cooking or request catering in the large modern kitchen.

The Wagon House, for day use only, is a meeting room that can accommodate forty people. A spa and swimming pool are available for all guests, and soft lawns throughout the grounds are perfect for reading and relaxing. A large library of videos on spiritual themes is found in the main house. Barbecues are also available for outdoor cooking and for day use by larger groups. Overnight rates are very reasonable, but the facilities are generally reserved for adults only, and no pets are allowed.

There are many trails through the surrounding hills for hiking, and the San Pablo National Wildlife Refuge, about twenty minutes away by car, is a fine place for bird-watching (especially waterfowl). The wine districts of Sonoma and Napa Valley are both less than an hour's drive away down two-lane country roads.

previous page: The water tower, once Mrs. Hearst's private painting studio, now accommodates two guests.

left: Silver Penny Farm, a gift of William Randolph Hearst II, overlooks the Petaluma River Valley.

The climate is mild, but there are definite seasons. During the winter and spring, flocks of sheep graze on lush green grass in the adjacent fields, a scene reminiscent of the English countryside. In late summer and fall, the fields grow dry, the tall grass by the roadside turns yellow, and the landscape returns once again to one of California.

top: The swimming pool is available for both overnight and day-use guests.

bottom: In spring, the countryside is almost English, but as summer approaches, the grass dies to a light brown and the scenery reverts to inland California.

Tall eucalyptus trees line the steep single-lane road from the main highway and mingle with redwoods, Monterey pines, and live oaks where the road flattens at the floor of Green Gulch. Gardens and terraced green fields spill westward on a gentle slope toward the Pacific Ocean for about a mile before they open onto John Muir Beach. To the east, the visitor sees only a vista of steep chaparral-covered hills that contain and embrace this unique farm, retreat center, and Zen community.

The Green Gulch Farm Zen Center was founded in 1972 after George Wheelwright sold 125 acres of his cattle ranch to the San Francisco Zen Center on the condition that it always remain in agriculture and be open to public access. Since that time, a dedicated group of American followers of the Soto Zen tradition have transformed the former ranch into a setting of peace and calming beauty.

The members of this community, follow a daily path of meditation, mindfulness, work, and service. "Sitting"—that is, sitting meditation, or *zazen*—leads these dedicated practitioners on a daily personal search toward an ever-deepening understanding of reality and compassion. "It's pretty hard not to notice zazen is changing your life," says one resident. "That's why we stay together—to help each other through the changes."

Green Gulch Farm Zen Center

1601 Shoreline Highway

Sausalito, California 94965

415/383-3134

Zen is not some kind of

excitement, but concentration

on our usual everyday routine.

—Shunryu Suzuki

The practice of zazen infuses life at Green Gulch with a palpable down-to-earth naturalness, an earthiness most clearly demonstrated in Green Gulch's two-acre formal garden and twelve-acre vegetable plots. The garden is inspired by and dedicated to Alan Chadwick, who introduced chemical-free growing techniques while at the University of Santa Cruz in the late 1960s and later lived and taught at Green Gulch Farm. The gardens are an easygoing combination of order and casual plantings laid out as a series of "rooms." Some rooms contain herb circles and strawberries, while others include apple, quince, and pear trees. Flowers, of course, abound throughout, and lush green lawns are perfect sites for leisurely picnics surrounded by freesias, ranunculuses, daffodils, and the gentle aroma of roses.

Green Gulch's organic vegetables—lettuce, chard, radicchio, broccoli, beets, and, come June, the exquisitely flavored rosefir apple fingerling potatoes—are highly prized in the area and supply Greens, the restaurant Zen Center started in San Francisco, as well as the Green Gulch community. The community once plowed these fields using horses in the farm's early years. Today, there are tractors, although it is not unusual to find a group of Zen students meditatively raking or hoeing in silence and concentration.

There is a variety of residential and guest programs at Green Gulch. Guest students stay at Cloud Hall, adjacent to the main meditation hall, and work on the property for part of each day. There are also intensive three-, five-, or seven-day meditation retreats (known as "sesshins")

previous page: The Lindisfarne Guest House was constructed using Japanese joinery techniques, with no nails whatsoever. Rooms share a balcony that overlooks the central thirty-foot-high atrium and its wood stove.

left: Furnishings in the guest rooms are simple, adequate, and immaculate.

held throughout the year. Practice retreats, requiring a minimum midweek stay of three nights, combine a private retreat with participation in the community's classes and activities. They cost very little.

Overnight guests, or those on a personal retreat, stay in the Lindisfarne Guest House, completed in 1983. Master carpenter Paul Discoe used classical Japanese joinery techniques on the structure— no nails were used in its construction—and the detailed finish carpentry inside is masterful. The guest house's twelve small rooms, arranged around a bright thirty-foot atrium, are small, but thanks to the generous use of white shades, all are filled with light. Each room has a double bed and a balcony or patio. In another guest facility, a separate suite with two rooms, a living room, and a kitchen is available for families. The cost for a night's stay in the guest house is comparable to reasonably priced bed and breakfasts in the area.

Overnight guests are invited to participate in the activities and classes of the community, but there are no formal requirements: Visitors are free to come and go as they please. Some stay at Green Gulch while on business in San Francisco, others choose to savor the peaceful atmosphere and relax amid the unhurried pace of the community. The setting and atmosphere at Green Gulch is comforting and safe. Occasionally, a well-known figure or celebrity may arrive for a few days of peace and anonymity. "They find it a good place just to be nobody," says one resident.

Easy hiking trails lead to adjoining parkland, including walks through Muir Woods and paths through the beauty of Mount Tamalpais State Park.

The food at Green Gulch is vegetarian (but includes milk and dairy products), organic, fresh, and wholesome. Bread is baked on the premises daily. Residents eat their meals together. Occasionally, the cuisine is graced by a delightful Japanese touch. There may, for instance, be seaweed among the carrots; however, the food is always familiar to the American palate.

Green Gulch is a highly sought after center for meetings, group retreats, and conferences for groups that require a setting for concentrated work, creative activity, and clear communications. Doctors and lawyers are among the many professional groups that hold meetings here. The Wheelwright Center and a new separate yurt-style building, the Selver House, can each accommodate a group of between twenty-five and forty, while the smaller library can handle a group of about fifteen.

A day visit to Green Gulch is a unique pleasure, but staying overnight reveals another of its many faces: that of a Zen temple with the monastic regimen of a community of dedicated seekers. In the cold predawn, the deep ringing of the temple bell fills the fog-shrouded valley, providing a focus for the meditators seated in the dark meditation hall. It is a pleasing sound, full of peace and clarity.

top: There are several buildings at Green Gulch for meetings. Here the Wheelwright Center and adjacent library are often used for groups of about thirty.

bottom: Green Gulch's ornamental gardens are laid out in thematic 'rooms.'

The renowned organic gardens at Green Gulch were inspired by and dedicated to Alan Chadwick, a pioneer in chemical-free growing techniques on the West Coast.

Hanging ginger and freshly baked bread await the day in Green Gulch's kitchen. "It's the hearth—and heart—of the community," says one member.

The zendo, or meditation
hall, is a former barn
reinforced by heavy over-
head beams to withstand
seismic forces. The white oak
and cedar used to fashion
the altar came from fallen
trees at Tassajara.

In the zazen posture, your mind and body

have great power to accept things as they

are, whether agreeable or disagreeable.

—Shunryu Suzuki

For miles along this stretch of the Big Sur coast, the steep Santa Lucia Mountains descend headlong toward the Pacific. There they meet the surf as a wall of high, stony cliffs, but at one point, forty-five miles south of Monterey, a wedge-shaped meadow clings to the edge of the continent. It was on this pocket of land off of the famed California State Route 1 that Esalen was founded, later to become one of the pioneering social and cultural forces in the country.

Once past the Esalen gatehouse, there are tall pines, ferns, and flower beds in a lush and sensuous display of vegetation. Low rows of shaded wooden cabins sit on narrow terraces, looking out onto a thick, broad lawn, a thriving vegetable garden, and a cool blue swimming pool. It is Eden in a nutshell. Then, like everywhere else along the Big Sur coast, comes the precipice and, eight stories below, a narrow black stony beach and the endless pounding of the waves. Halfway down the cliffs, at the southern end of the property, is a steep path to the bathhouse and the hot springs. For centuries, these springs were sacred to the Esalen tribe, Native Americans who inhabited this part of Big Sur. For the past three decades, these dress-optional baths perched above the Pacific have been visited by

Esalen Institute

Big Sur, California 93920-9616

408/667-3000

tens of thousands of visitors and are still considered to be sacred, albeit in a far looser sense.

A dozen guests at a time can enjoy the famous long-stroke Esalen massages in the open air. Other visitors take a break from their challenging seminars to sink into the healing sulfurous waters to socialize, meditate, or simply gaze out at the ocean below and marvel at the silvered flash of a dolphin leaping through the gray-blue waves.

But Esalen is more than just a setting of natural and healing beauty. When residents on this cliffside community speak of the famed "Esalen environment," they are referring to a state of mind as much as a sense of place. Esalen is where people come to change the quality of their lives.

The 125-acre property was bought in 1910 by Dr. Henry Murphy, who planned to establish a European-style spa. Following his death, his wife developed the site as a modest tourist establishment. In 1961, her grandson Michael Murphy and his friend Richard Price, two Stanford graduates, leased the land and founded the institute that would become a renowned seminal forum for examining subjects dealing with the synthesis between intuition and intellect, body and mind.

In its early days, cultural luminaries like Henry Miller, Alan Watts, and Aldous Huxley would drop by and teach seminars. Cutting-edge psychologists like Abraham Maslow and Fritz Perls developed their Gestalt and encounter techniques at Esalen. The institute may have

been run somewhat haphazardly during those formative years, but there was a palpable sense of experiment, adventure, and breakthrough.

Many of the ideas developed and forged at Esalen in the fields of holistic health, body work, psychic awareness, and nonverbal communication have quietly been absorbed into the mainstream. Today, the institute continues to be just a little ahead of the cultural curve, although, as it enters midlife, Esalen has mellowed somewhat.

previous page: An oceanside trail leads to the bathhouse and the famed Esalen hot springs, named after the Native American tribe that once lived on this coast.

left: Accommodations at Esalen are rustic and simple. Here, a loft space for a family-sized group.

Esalen now runs like clockwork, with an efficient and professional staff of seventy that includes a massage crew of twenty-eight. There is also a full-scale child-care facility—the Gazebo School Park facility—used by residents and guests alike.

Esalen continues to offer dozens of courses, ranging in duration from a weekend to a month, cover subjects in the arts, ecology, shamanic processes, intellectual play, martial arts, and psychological processes, among others. The seminar "Experiencing Esalen," held several times a year, is recommended for newcomers. The fees for seminars and workshops, which include tuition, food, and lodging, are moderately expensive, and only limited scholarship assistance is available.

Several separate meeting rooms are available on the property, each with its own distinctive character. Smaller buildings, such as Rolf (for Ida) and Fritz (for Perls), hold groups of twenty to thirty people; the Big House is used for larger groups.

Accommodations at Esalen are clean, simple, and comfortable.

Typically, the wooden cabins, which may have shared bathroom facilities, have two beds. There are also rooms with bunk beds, housing three or more visitors, and sleeping bag space for other workshop participants. Room and board only, without a seminar, is usually available midweek and on some weekends.

For a deeper sense of the Esalen environment, there are residence and work scholarship programs for stays of one month or longer.

The food at Esalen is excellent: fresh, healthful, and tasty. The mostly vegetarian cuisine (some chicken and turkey is offered) is served cafeteria-style in the main lodge, a low comfortable building with an outdoor patio. Most of the produce is from Esalen's own organic vegetable gardens.

With up to 220 people at a time on the grounds, Esalen can resemble a cross between a country club and a college campus. Yet, scattered throughout the property there are dozens of quiet places to which you can escape. Some overlook the ocean, others are hidden in shaded glens by a small waterfall. They all offer a setting for quiet meditation and reflection and are as much a part of the Esalen mystique and the Esalen environment as the many enriching seminars.

With all these benefits and attractions, Esalen is not to be forgotten. "People come here," says one staff member, "and take a piece of it back in their hearts."

At Esalen, there are always quiet places to escape for solitude and reflection.

The swimming pool, perched on the edge of the continent, overlooks the Pacific Ocean.

top: Eden in a nutshell, a seamless mix of the wild and the cultivated.

left: The Big House, built on the edge of the precipice, was the original residence of the Murphy family, owners of the property. Today, renovated throughout, it is a popular setting for some of the larger seminars held at Esalen.

At New Camaldoli, overlooking the Big Sur coast, a large hermitage continues a tradition of solitude and community that stretches back almost nine hundred years to a small town in northern Tuscany. "We're a contemplative house," says one brother. "People here really dig in and take it seriously. But," he adds, "we feel that everyone is contemplative at some level. Here, they can touch that."

Set on the side of a mountain overlooking the rugged coastline, the eight hundred acres of the hermitage's property include groves of dense old-growth redwood forest that still bear the scars of a wildfire that ravaged these hills in 1988. Beyond the dark trees, the view westward is all light: a phalanx of chaparral-covered slopes that plummet three thousand feet to meet the cold waters of the Pacific Ocean in a fine white line of surf and spray.

The former ranch was purchased in 1958 by the Camaldese order, a Benedictine branch combining the solitary and communal aspects of monasticism in both monasteries and hermitages. The buildings and the layout "were designed to express mystery and the ineffable," says one brother. "We," he adds, "fill out the space."

New Camaldoli Hermitage

Big Sur, California 93920

408/667-2456

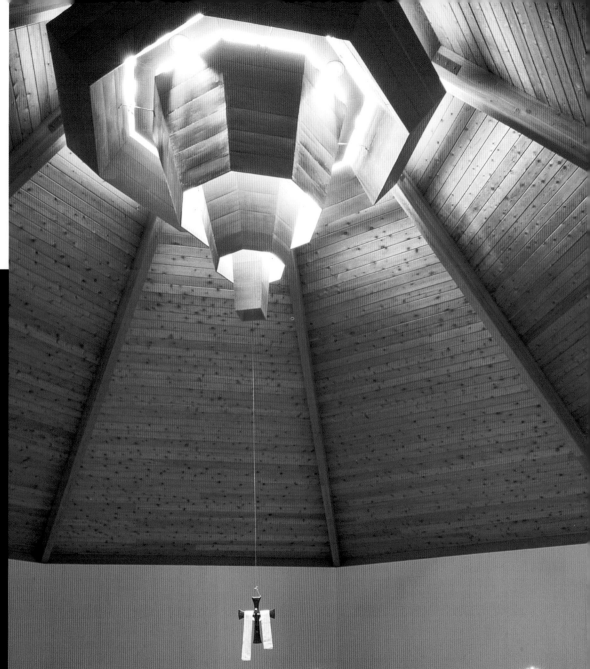

Empty yourself and sit waiting.
Sit in your cell as in paradise.
Put the whole world behind you
and forget it.
—Saint Romuald, inspirer of
Camaldese Benedictine life

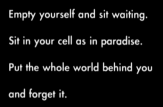

Some twenty-six monks live in small cottages, each with its own small chapel and garden. At present, two monks are recluses—the closest a community member can come to complete solitude within the hermitage structure. But all members of this community lead lives of solitude and community, "cultivating," according to one brother, "a deepening awareness of God's presence in all, through all, and embracing all."

As at all Benedictine monasteries, guests are warmly welcomed, however, the hermitage's emphasis on both solitude and community is carried through in the arrangement of the guests' quarters and their contact with the monks and other guests. Spiritual direction may be requested, and there is always a monk available at the well-stocked bookstore and Guest Center. Guests are requested to maintain the atmosphere of quiet in certain areas. They are also invited, but not required, to join with the brothers in their four daily times of prayer and worship in the strikingly simple church. The Eucharist, a central focus of the community, is celebrated in the impressive rotunda renovated in 1976 by Polish architect Frank Kazmarcik.

previous page: California sunlight streams through the eyecatching baldachin in the rotunda, used exclusively for celebrating the Eucharist.

left: Walks through the grounds lead to ocean vistas and aged oaks.

Long-term guests—staying from one week to a month—are lodged in four fully self-contained house trailers nestled into the hill, each trailer with its own wooden sun deck. For short-term stays, there are nine simple rooms, each with its own garden patio overlooking the ocean, in a cinder block building with a common kitchen. A simple but filling vegetarian lunch—often with an Italian flair—is supplied by the monastery's kitchen and eaten privately. Breakfasts and dinners are prepared by guests in the common kitchen.

The setting at New Camaldoli inspires quiet and insight, for despite the minimal contact most guests have with the monks, their presence is felt everywhere. Many deep and long-lasting friendships have bloomed at New Camaldoli. "The brothers have a gentle, loving approach," says one guest. "They invite you into the contemplative life."

Some of the hermitage grounds are open to guests. The steep, serpentine two-mile-long driveway that climbs from the stony beach through the lush hillside growth has spectacular views at every turn. The redwood groves in the nearby canyon are also available for walking, and scattered throughout the property are benches, ideal locations for quiet meditation and introspection.

Sunsets at New Camaldoli are magnificent, but it is worth the effort to greet the dawn and look down upon the thick blanket of white fog that often rolls in from the west, covering the bay below. "Some mornings, there's a deep blue sky and a bowl full of clouds," says one brother. "It makes you feel like you must be in Heaven."

top: The hexagonal roofs of the monks' cottages resemble cells in a beehive. At their center, the church.

bottom: A quiet pool at the edge of a redwood forest in the heart of Big Sur.

The legend of the origin of the springs at Tassajara is timeless.

A powerful chief once tended his sick sister in this narrow gorge, but despite his great medicine, her condition worsened. Heartbroken, the chief threw himself on the earth and turned to stone, from which issued hot tears that cured the young girl.

Geologists no doubt have less mythic explanations for the springs' origins, but they agree that the waters at Tassajara (which means "the place where meat is cured by drying") are exceptional. At 135 to 140 degrees Fahrenheit, they are the hottest in the nation and also the richest of any in mineral content, according to the Smithsonian Institution.

Charles Quilty bought the former hunting lodge in 1884 and built the fourteen-mile-long road from Jamesburg to bring visitors to Monterey County's first resort. General Sherman and Ignace Paderewski were among the thousands who came "to take the waters," as visiting a spa was then known.

Fires ravaged the resort more than once. Tassajara went through a series of owners and fell upon increasingly hard times. In 1946, Joan Crawford's ex-husband leased the land, tried to make the property pay, and failed. The owners in the 1960s kept Tassajara

Tassajara Reservation Office

300 Page Street

San Francisco, California 94102

415/431-3771

No need here to do,

to accomplish, to produce

—it is enough to walk, to read,

to breathe easily and rest

assured, and, of course, to eat.

—Edward Espe Brown, *The*

Tassajara Recipe Book

limping along and advertised it accurately as "not everyone's resort. No TV. No radio. No fog."

Tassajara's fortunes changed in 1967, when the 160-acre plot was purchased by followers of the Zen master Shunryu Suzuki. Their pioneering vision, to establish the first Zen monastery in the nation, did not include running a resort, but many longtime visitors to Tassajara demanded that the hot springs be kept open to the public. The newly founded monastery agreed to operate the resort from May to September, now known as the "guest season."

Tassajara today is an easygoing, yet meticulously run, operation, but it is still "not everyone's resort." The road from Jamesburg is a test for both gearbox and brakes (there is a daily four-wheel-drive "stage" for the fainthearted); there is no electricity for guests, let alone television; and the accommodations are simple and rustic. However, for the thousands who choose to come here each year, Tassajara provides just what they need: a resort in natural surroundings and an ambience that is calming, focused, and healing.

There is a sense of seamless balance between the natural and the constructed at Tassajara; everything just happens to be in the perfect place. No music is allowed in the valley, so the soothing sound of Tassajara Creek rushing over its rocky bed is a constant background for the birdsong and occasional ringing of bells from the *zendo*, the meditation hall. Butterflies and hummingbirds flit among the branches of alder, sycamore, and big-leaf maple, while green stalks of newly planted bamboo about the cabins lend a decidedly Asian element to the setting.

There is room for eighty guests at this green oasis. They all show up for meals, but for the rest of the day, the scores of guests seem to disappear completely. Some sleep for days in their rooms. Others go hiking in the adjacent wilderness and park areas. Many linger or read on the lush grassy areas or spend quiet afternoons by the side of the spring-fed swimming pool or at the water hole a short walk downriver.

Many guests, of course, head straight for the bathhouses, recently relocated for seismic safety reasons at a cost of about half a million dollars. The new bathhouses are an unassuming blend of function, simplicity, and grace. The separate men's and women's sides each have warm gray tiles in the main baths that blend immaculately with the surrounding rocks. The stream is steps away, available for a cold plunge.

previous page: The taiko drum outside the meditation hall is used to call community members to formal zazen and to announce work periods.

left: Tassajara grows its own flowers. Colorful sprays and bouquets often grace the tables at mealtimes.

Guests stay in a variety of unadorned accommodations, from dormitories and wooden Japanese cabins with shared bathrooms to a two-room suite in a stone building with its own deck. Prices for a night's stay are moderately expensive—less so during weekdays—but no one complains because the rates also include three meals of the renowned Tassajara cooking.

Tassaraja cookbooks have sold well above half a million copies, and with good reason: the food at Tassajara is heavenly. "What goes into our cooking," writes Edward Espe Brown, author of some of the cookbooks, "is generosity more than genius, kindness more than creativity." At Tassajara, everything, from breads and salads to entrees of stuffed red pepper, tofu brochettes, or chili rellenos soufflé, comes to the table in a state of gastronomical perfection. Lunch is served buffet-style and is eaten at picnic tables beneath a grape arbor in the outdoor dining area. Dinner is a sit-down affair in the dining room at tables lit by kerosene lamps, with Zen students as waiters.

A community of forty residents (seventy in the summer) runs the resort, and even during the height of the guest season, community members rise at 5:30 A.M. for the first of several sessions of zazen—sitting meditation—facing a white wall in mindful attention for an hour at a time. Several five-day retreats open to the public are held during the guest season on subjects ranging from "Cooking as a Spiritual Practice" to Deep Ecology and Buddhism. But after Labor Day, Tassajara reverts to a Soto Zen monastery with no guests at all. During the winter, residents spend the bulk of their waking hours, including meals, inside the zendo pursuing their demanding spiritual practice. "You're put inside a bamboo tube," said one longtime resident, "and then you see what your distractions are." Zazen "softens you, opens you up. The end result is a warm, compassionate, and spontaneous human being." Not to mention superb hosts and sublime cooks.

top: The swimming pool offers a view of the surrounding Ventana Wilderness.

bottom: The breakfast buffet always includes a selection of Tassajara's famous breads.

The awareness that you are here, right

now, is the ultimate fact.

—Shunryu Suzuki

One of the many settings for resting, reading, or just sitting at Tassajara. The hand-hewn furniture was crafted by J. B. Blanc.

A stone Buddha sits contentedly beside a rustic bench. In the background, a guest house is nestled among the trees.

Mount Calvary is a monastery well suited to higher thoughts.
The narrow road from the Santa Barbara Mission is both steep and winding, and the final half mile is a lonely stretch of blacktop that clings defiantly to the side of the mountain. Once on it, there is no turning back. Like a pilgrim of yore, the visitor to Mount Calvary must persevere, but the ascent is well rewarded. Stepping from the car, the visitor to this mountaintop sanctuary is greeted by a magnificent panorama of the Santa Barbara coast, a view that enhances the feeling that one has indeed left all cares and worries far below.

That feeling of distance from the mundane is promoted by the friendly brothers of the Order of the Holy Cross, an Episcopal (Anglican) monastic community, who gladly share their beautiful grounds and monastery with visitors of all denominations. People come here for many reasons, but the monastery is best suited, according to one of the community members, "to the kind of person who has reached a point in their life where they know they have to make important decisions." Weekends are often booked by church groups, twelve-step groups—Alcoholics Anonymous, for example—and others. Weekdays are better suited for the individual who needs some quiet time to focus on his or her innermost needs in the company of an amiable monastic community.

Mount Calvary Retreat House

2500 Mount Calvary Road

Santa Barbara, California 93105

805/962-9855

Wisdom builds a house, under-

standing establishes a home.

—Proverbs 24:3

Far from being pietistic and standoffish, the members of this community are approachable and gregarious, recognizing that the dynamic that evolves between guests and members is a crucial part of any retreat here. And while discussions can turn eventually to matters of theology, they may just as easily cover subjects as mundane as gardening, current affairs, or a recent film.

"When people are with us," says one monk, "let it be their home. We only ask that our guests respect our life." Four times each day the sonorous bell in the courtyard tolls to announce the daily prayer offices (and morning Eucharist) in the small chapel, a converted ballroom. Visitors are invited, but not required, to attend. The Grand Silence following compline extends from 10:00 P.M. until 8:00 A.M. the following morning; guests are requested at these hours to maintain a reasonable quiet.

previous page: The original house, built in 1928 on a peak of the Santa Ynez Mountains, commands a 360-degree panorama of the city of Santa Barbara, the ocean, and the mountains.

left: The bell used for calling the brothers to prayer frames the view down the coast, here looking southeast.

The Spanish revival–style house, built in 1928, was not designed as a monastery, but the long corridors and small quadrangle give an immediate sense of a cloistered community in the European tradition. The Guest House features a large common room for meetings, a sunporch for watching the spectacular sunsets, and three separate libraries, one each for books on literature, scripture, and theology.

The order purchased the structure in 1947 and has made several improvements since then to the main house and the gardens on the twenty-acre property. Over the years, friends of the monastery have donated a multitude of gifts and many rare antiques, including Spanish colonial masterpieces that fill the galleria by the main entrance and a collection of priceless Navajo blankets, selections of which hang in each of the guest rooms.

Sleeping accommodations are simple, with nineteen rooms (eleven with double beds, eight with single beds), each of which features breathtaking views of the vista or garden below. Suggested donations are reasonable and include all meals, which are tasty. The members of the community take great pride in the variety of homemade bread they bake to accompany the food, which is often inspired by the traditions of Mexican cuisine. Meals in the small refectory are congenial affairs, except for breakfast, the sole repast eaten in silence.

Located at an elevation of 1,200 feet, Mount Calvary is in the heart of the coastal sage ecosystem. In spring, the surrounding hills and the backdrop of the Santa Ynez Mountains to the north are carpeted in green and punctuated by wildflowers. But these mountains are drier than most along the coast in southern California, and come summer, the land turns tawny and the air is heavy with the aromatic smell of sage, chemise, and other species of the hillside chaparral.

Looking down from this mountaintop setting onto the city of Santa Barbara, the endless expanse of the Pacific Ocean, and the grand sweep of the coast to both the north and south, it is easy to understand why Mount Calvary is, indeed, an inspiring environment for anyone seeking clarity of thought and a different way of viewing their life. "The vista," said one brother, displaying the panorama that this community enjoys every day, "can help put everything into perspective."

top: Simple frescoes outline the main entrance.

bottom: An iron cross in the drought-tolerant monastery garden, a gift of the Dupont family, carries brass symbols of the Passion.

There are three separate libraries and reading areas at Mt. Calvary. This, the most spacious, also serves as a meeting area.

The galleria holds a wealth of artwork, including antique furniture, several paintings, and, at the rear, an ornate gilded altarpiece crafted in Peru in the 1740s.

"This is a most healing place," says one of the Immaculate Heart Community members, "because of the beauty of it." Indeed, the elegant two-story building that houses this unique spiritual renewal center lies cloistered in the heart of a green paradise set in a fertile mountain canyon. Groves of live oaks, flowering acacias, and sycamores shade the gently rolling grounds. Opposite the center's baronial entrance is an orchard of almost biblical variety. In spring, the branches of the fruit trees are rife with blossoms, and come the latter days of summer, they are heavy with ripe loquats, nectarines, avocados, and figs.

Behind the house to the north, the imposing profile of Montecito Peak stands against a pellucid blue sky. Even on the hottest days, afternoon sea breezes from the Pacific Ocean wander up the narrow San Ysidro Canyon, cooling this gentle and quiet Eden.

Almost two centuries ago, Spanish padres built a small way station close to this site for missionaries traveling up and down the coast. The present structure is of much more recent vintage. Originally designed in the 1920s for an oil magnate, the house was purchased by the Sisters of the Immaculate Heart of Los Angeles in 1943 to be converted into a novitiate. In 1970, the sisters chose as a group to cease being a religious order and became the Immaculate Heart

Immaculate Heart Community Center

888 San Ysidro Lane

Santa Barbara, California 93108

805/969-2474

La Casa de Maria

805/969-5031

74

We harvest the fruit of hope to

begin again to hope.

—Corita Kent, late artist and

member of the community

Community. Four years later, the classic Spanish revival–style house was designated a center for spiritual renewal.

The main house is as captivating as the grounds that surround it. The imposing walls are built of stone quarried from a nearby creek, the floors are fashioned of pegged local oak, the fireplaces bear facades imported from Italy, the bathrooms feature tiles from Spain and Czechoslovakia, and the ceilings of the main bedrooms are intricate constructions of Siamese teak.

The furniture throughout is donated, so a Baker chest of drawers or a mint-condition Chippendale dining table may be found in the same room as an entirely unprepossessing sofa or chair of far less elegant provenance. This mixture of the refined and the prosaic gives the center's furnishings and decorations a unique charm—a definite sense of home that is unpretentious, welcoming, and easy to live in.

previous page: Classic wrought ironwork frames a door looking onto the central courtyard.

left: The stately vestibule of the main guest house. The dream of an oil-magnate, no expense was spared in building this classic Spanish revival-style mansion.

The center requires nothing more from guests than a desire to experience the serenity of the setting and to respect the peace of others. There are no bells, no expectations, and no demands. Meals—both non-vegetarian and vegetarian—are prepared from scratch, often using vegetables from the garden and fruits from the orchard. Breakfast and lunch are easygoing "pick-up" affairs: at their leisure, guests choose from the foods and dishes provided. Dinner, an important focus of the day, is eaten together and served family-style, providing an opportunity for sharing thoughts and insights. An optional ecumenical service held after dinner is both simple and spontaneous in nature. The extensive library is well stocked with a wide variety of books and audio tapes.

There are six large bedrooms for guests, each with a private bath, and accommodations are available from Wednesday through Sunday afternoon. A separate three-bedroom hermitage, suitable for writers and scholars seeking solitude, is also available. The suggested fees for both single visitors and married couples is reasonable. Reservations must be made well ahead and a two-day minimum stay is required.

La Casa de Maria, the adjoining retreat center, occupies seven acres of the grounds and hosts some thiteen thousand participants a year who come for interfaith gatherings or to learn about healing practices, sensory awareness, recovery from alcoholism, and the like. Facilities at La Casa de Maria include a 150-seat chapel, meeting rooms, a lounge, gift shop, and a cafeteria-style dining room. Accommodations are in simple but well-fashioned retreat rooms whose Mission-style architecture blends surprisingly well into the woodsy setting.

Guests at the main house are welcome to use La Casa de Maria's facilities, including the pool, tennis courts, and massage rooms. Of special interest is the hushed meditation chapel lit only by sunlight streaming through hundreds of holes that form a cross-circle mandala on the small structure's south wall.

Meditation and quiet are encouraged but not required during visits to the Center for Spiritual Renewal. Visitors may appreciate a walk through the orchard or enjoy catching a glimpse of the Pacific Ocean through the palms and oaks.

The center welcomes women and men of all faiths who seek a place of peace and renewal of spirit.

top: Built in a similar Spanish revival-style, the adjacent La Casa de Maria hosts group retreats.

bottom: A concrete sculpture commemorates the appearance of Our Lady of Fatimah before two young girls and a boy.

The winding dirt road to the Ojai Foundation ends abruptly at the crest of a ridge. Miles away, the tawny strata of the wind-worn Topa Topa Ridge stand high to the north, surrounded on either side by endless expanses of chaparral. Far below are the flat green fields of the Ojai River Valley.

In 1927, Annie Besant, president of the Theosophist Society, stood under an oak tree on this same ridge, then purchased the four hundred acres and established the Happy Valley Foundation. In 1975, forty of the easternmost acres were leased to Human Dimensions Institute/West, an organization that was exploring the relationship between science and spirituality.

The institute was later renamed the Ojai Foundation, and under the guidance of its first director, Dr. Joan Halifax, an anthropologist, the foundation achieved a broader and more earthy vision, offering seminars on subjects ranging from ecology and shamanism to Native American ceremonies and performing arts workshops. Robert Bly, Thich Nhat Hanh, and R. D. Laing are among those who have led gatherings at the rustic foundation.

Today, the Ojai Foundation is still an educational sanctuary and site for retreats, both group and individual, with a mission that continues to evolve but remains rooted in a deep respect for the land.

Ojai Foundation

P.O. Box 1620

Ojai, California 93024

805/646-0902

"Ojai Foundation? It's a place where East meets West in the wilderness."
—Resident

"Our connection with the Earth is our center," says one long-term resident. "The land is our teacher."

The natural setting, less than two hours from Los Angeles, both inspires and calms. Red-tailed hawks soar overhead. Deer, bobcats, and coyotes still scurry through the bush in the surrounding hills. The foundation's land itself is a semiwilderness, varying from bright sunlit fields and gardens to mysterious wooded glens.

Facilities throughout are rudimentary—wooden yurts, graceful tepees, and canvas domes are used for lodging. Civilized amenities are available, but they never dominate: hot and cold running water and flush toilets, for instance, may require a few minutes' walk along a narrow trail among the oaks. "There's a self-sufficiency we expect of those who visit," says one member. Yet, even those who neither expected nor are used to the rustic approach, end up charmed by a few days stripped of the gloss of civilization.

A massive live oak—the Learning Tree—spreads its protective branches over the most popular classroom on the site. Other meeting sites are also designed to impact the terrain as little as possible. Two kivas are dug into the earth with a fireplace at their center. Larger, more modern structures, such as the Community Yurt, can hold up to thirty people, the upper limit of the number of people the foundation can accommodate for a group retreat. One limiting factor is the communal kitchen that serves the needs of both groups and individuals. Meals are eaten outside, overlooking the valley.

There are two small gardens—one for herbs, another for vegetables—that supply some of the produce, and a smattering of fruit trees that provide persimmons, figs, plums, and tangerines.

A walk along the land's many trails reveals a large seated Buddha, a small Christian shrine, and a Native American medicine wheel, indications of the ecumenical nature of the foundation and the eclectic range of activities and retreats it supports and hosts. The sweat lodge at the Ojai Foundation is another form of shrine, and still smaller shrines abound. "People have created sacred places everywhere on the land," says one staff member. Over the years, regular visitors to the foundation have discovered their special spots on the land and blessed them with prayers, ceremonies, and memorials. Some of these personal shrines may be as modest as a small mound of pebbles or a single abalone shell left upturned among the leaves.

previous page: The foundation's land sits on the edge of the narrow Upper Ojai Valley. Here, looking south to Sulphur Mountain.

left: A yurt, a Mongolian dwelling of latticed frameworks and a domed canvas top, sits among the California live oaks.

Foundation studies—weekend programs covering council training, mindfulness, storytelling, and permaculture—are held in April and October and often introduce first-time visitors to the message of the foundation.

The climate in this part of California can be extreme. In the winter, temperatures fall to the thirties at night, and rain can be torrential. In the summer, temperatures often rise above 100 degrees Fahrenheit, the grass turns brown, and creeks are reduced to bare trickles.

Individuals seeking to live at the foundation for up to a month at a time are encouraged to come at any season and can defray the bulk of the modest costs by working twenty-five hours a week. Day visitors are welcomed at no charge, but should check first with the staff.

Accommodations are reasonably priced for individuals or couples who stay overnight in any of the structures, and camping on the land is inexpensive. A five-day stay is recommended "to get a flavor of the land."

A new emphasis is placed on the Ojai Foundation's programs for school children. Sixth graders come from the city and stay for two days in the Children's Grove, playing, working, and learning to connect with the earth in a meaningful way. High school seniors come for five-day rite-of-passage retreats that include sweat lodge ceremonies.

The sweat lodge ceremony is a central feature of the Ojai Foundation and available for adults, too. Native American elders and shamans make regular visits to the foundation's land to lead the ancient ceremonies of healing and cleansing. Seated on the bare earth, amid the steamy darkness, glowing rocks, and the scent of sage, those within chant and speak their heart with one another. It is a powerful ceremony and, like the Ojai Foundation itself, simple and rooted in the earth.

Pottery from the outdoor ceramics studio (bottom) is sometimes fired over open flames in the classic Native American-style.

The light-filled interior of a guest yurt. While comfortable during the hot summers, they can be chilly during other seasons.

All the masters tell us that the reality of life—which our noisy waking consciousness prevents us from hearing—speaks to us chiefly in silence.

—Karlfried Graf Dürckheim

Spiny Joshua trees and yucca plants greet the visitor who leaves the hot plains of the western Mojave Desert and drives into the San Gabriel Mountains to reach Saint Andrew's Abbey. The entrance is hard to miss: "No hunting except for peace," reads their sign by the side of the road.

The abbey is on a former ranch, and signs of its agricultural past are everywhere. The modest wooden chapel, center of the community's life, was once a stable; the ceramics studio is located in a former milking barn; some of the twenty monks live in a former cow barn, and one monk's room is a transformed pig sty.

But there are new buildings, too. The spacious lounge, a site for lectures and meetings, is adjacent to the high, vaulted refectory, with its tall window looking onto Joshua and juniper trees. A short walk to the cool waters of an artificial pond reveals a teahouse and some Chinese inscriptions, clues to the background of the monks who created this oasis of peace.

Saint Andrew's Abbey
31001 N. Valyermo Road
P.O. Box 40
Valyermo, California 93563
805/944-2178

The abbey was founded in 1956 by nine Chinese and European Benedictine monks who had been expelled by the Communists in 1952 from their monastery in Chengtu, China. Destitute, the monks came to America and spent three years searching for a new home for their community. The ranch fulfilled all their criteria: it was close to

For I have learned,

in whatsoever state I am,

therewith to be content.

—St. Paul, Philippians 4:11

Los Angeles but smog-free, had an excellent well, "and," emphasizes Father Vincent, who found the land, "the price was $99,000 for three hundred acres—and everything on it."

Remnants of the congregation's former life in the Far East can still be found at Saint Andrew's. The intricately crafted monstrance used on Mondays bears the Chinese ideogram for heaven, and several silk vestments with Asian embroidery hang beside the plain white albs the monks don to celebrate the Eucharist.

The fact that the land sat squarely atop the San Andreas Fault, the most important of the many active earthquake fault lines in California, only strengthened the monks' faith. "We took the name Saint Andrew's," says one monk referring to the anglicized version of the fault's name, "to give us a little extra coverage."

Today, the abbey occupies 760 acres and includes fields that once held abundant fruit trees. "We were all militant scholars and linguists, not really orchardists," admits one resident. The twenty brothers who live here today continue their intellectual heritage, teaching and lecturing on music and the arts as well as in many fields of religious knowledge.

A variety of seminars, workshops, and retreats are offered at Saint Andrew's throughout the year. Subjects studied range from the works of Thomas Merton to sacred dance to Christian chant in contemplative prayer. The Annual Fall Festival attracts showings from artists and craftspersons throughout the West, and on Sundays, many worshipers from the nearby burgeoning desert communities arrive for midday mass.

Guests are free to join in the religious rhythm of monastic life, but beyond the expectation of a quiet and respectful comportment, nothing else is required of them. The simple but substantial food is served buffet-style in the vaulted refectory. As at most Benedictine monasteries, the Grand Silence lasts from evening until after breakfast, but lunch and dinner can be lively events with an easygoing interchange between cloister and guests at the long tables.

The ceramic studio produces and sells a wide range of hand-crafted religious images and angels that are both childlike and charming in design. There is also a secondhand bookstore and an extensive library with over twenty-five thousand volumes, including many by and about the church fathers and mystics.

The dormitory building is made of concrete blocks and consists of seventeen unadorned rooms, each with two beds. Suggested donations for a night's stay and three meals are reasonable. The adjacent Youth Center, built on a former turkey ranch, is a completely separate facility and can handle groups of seventy-seven in boys' and girls' dorms.

previous page: The San Andreas Fault, source of the abbey's name, runs directly under the property after it veers out of the Mojave Desert in the distance, and heads up through the San Gabriel Mountains.

top: Crosses mark the last resting place of community members among the Joshua trees, a species of the yucca that often grows in odd-looking "groves" as below.

There are many hiking trails through the adjacent national park, and a small path on the abbey's land leads guests through a desert-style version of the stations of the cross.

Saint Andrew's can be a busy center of activity, but during the week—and always at night—the cleansing serenity of the high desert returns. Many guests on programmed retreats often discover something at Saint Andrew's they never expected and return to find it again, privately. "It is a deepening, a movement towards," says one monk of his own personal search. "A movement that seems to have no end." For so many other seekers, the stark desert provides an appropriate setting for entering into that infinite movement and, in the process, finding a sense of inner peace and spiritual renewal. "In the desert," notes one monk, "there isn't anywhere to hide."

top: The refectory window looks onto the Joshua trees and junipers of the high desert setting.

bottom: A shaded walkway beside the main building.

Malibu is perhaps best known for the many celebrities who live along this expensive stretch of the Pacific coast. But Malibu is also rugged mountains, and perched on one of them, high above the famed beaches, is a jewel of a retreat house that offers the kind of peace, solitude, and stillness that no amount of money can buy.

The setting of Serra Retreat is spectacular. To the north, the deeply incised Malibu Canyon winds its way into the steep inclines of the chaparral-covered Santa Monica Mountains. To the south, directly below the retreat, the canyon abruptly opens to the Pacific in a broad green swath of sycamores, willows, and ferns that all but hide the meandering Malibu Creek and the lagoon that marks its arrival at the Pacific Ocean.

"Yon Boundless Ocean is the best symbol of eternity," wrote Frederick Hastings Rindge, who bought Rancho Malibu in 1892 and built his Victorian ranch house not far from the retreat's present location. Rindge died in 1905, and in 1929, his widow, May Rindge, chose the summit of a nearby hill as the site for a fifty-room Mediterranean mansion. No expense was spared on constructing what came to be known as "The Castle on the Hill." Rindge even established her own pottery factory on a nearby beach to supply the

Serra Retreat

3401 Serra Road

P.O. Box 127

Malibu, California 90265

310/456-6631

Observe how the lilies of the field grow; they do not toil nor do they spin, yet I say to you that even Solomon in all his glory did not clothe himself like one of these.

—Matthew 6:28-29

exquisite hand-painted tiles that would decorate every room. Bankruptcy prevented the "castle's" completion, and following May Rindge's death in 1942, the Franciscan order bought the house and twenty-six acres of land for $50,000.

The site, renamed Serra Hill, was originally meant to be a seminary, but a year after its purchase, the order chose to establish a retreat center for laypeople instead. Over the next three decades, the Franciscans added new structures, planted trees, and created carefully designed gardens. In time, the Serra Retreat served as a refuge of peace and serenity for laypeople and clergy alike. The brothers also completed the meticulous task of tiling the unfinished rooms in the main house with the inventory of carefully stored tiles.

In 1970, barely four years after the retreat's new chapel had been dedicated, a devastating wildfire swept down from the mountains, burning tens of thousands of acres of land throughout Malibu. Firefighters were unable to stop its advance, and when the firestorm exploded over the adjacent ridges, it incinerated the original Rindge house, with the exception of a few basement rooms.

In the years following that devastating fire, many new buildings were added to the retreat, and on the Feast of Saint Francis of Assisi, in October 1993, the brothers joyfully dedicated a new glass-walled chapel topped by a wrought iron cross that had been salvaged from the ruins of the gutted main house twenty-three years before. Barely two weeks after the chapel's dedication, another firestorm raced through the tinder-dry Malibu chaparral and, once again fed by powerful desert winds,

reached the mouth of Malibu Canyon. Anxious friars watched from the safety of the beach as thick black smoke and walls of flame 150 feet high crested the ridge to the north and raced toward Serra Hill. When dawn broke, the hill and the mountains around it were a charred and smoldering moonscape, but thanks to the courageous efforts of firefighters, the retreat's buildings stood virtually unharmed, although its trees and gardens suffered severe damage.

previous page: The statue of Junipero Serra, founder of the California missions, stands on "The Point," overlooking Malibu Creek, the famed sandy beaches, and the Pacific Ocean.

left: Flowers and gardens abound on the retreat's property. Tiles salvaged from the devastating fire of 1970 are used throughout as decoration, as above, surrounding the arched windows in a recent addition.

Since then, the retreat's gardens have been brought back to their acclaimed beauty, and the Fatimah shrine, one of the few parts of the retreat lost to the flames, has been rebuilt and replanted.

Today, the retreat, with five friars and a staff of fifteen, continues its busy year-round schedule of hosting some ten thousand people who come here in groups and as private individuals. The facilities are open to a wide variety of denominations and nonprofit groups, from city councilpersons, to university boards of regents, Jewish organizations, and, of course, many Catholic groups—including the quarterly convocation of the local province of the Franciscan order.

There are five meeting rooms and an outside area beside the main lounge with a spectacular view of the mountains and ocean. Many of the group retreats at Serra are hosted by renowned presenters, such as Father Emery Tang, and cover enrichment weekends for caregivers, those who are divorced and separated, couples, and Hispanic fathers and sons, among others. Many individuals of all denominations choose to stay at Serra in midweek. "A retreat at Serra allows you to take a look at your spiritual life," says one brother. "We want people to ask themselves the difficult questions while they're here."

Accommodations for up to a hundred people are in modern and comfortable rooms with views of the mountains, coastline, or courtyard gardens. Healthful meals—a light cuisine with only an occasional red-meat entree—are cooked from scratch in the kitchen and served cafeteria-style in the bright and airy dining room. Favorite dishes at Serra include a variety of fresh salads, chili rellenos, and the continental breakfast and brunch on Sundays. Wine is served on Saturday nights; coffee and tea is on tap twenty-four hours a day. Suggested fees for group retreats are modest; rates for individual midweek retreats are moderate.

The setting, less than an hour from downtown Los Angeles, lends itself to a spiritual experience and nurtures creative focus. At every turn, there are viewpoints with captivating vistas. The most popular by far is "The Point," a prowlike outcropping facing south, where a statue of Junípero Serra, the seventeenth-century founder of the mission chain in California whose name graces the retreat, presides over the panorama of the famed coastline and, on clear days, of the island of Santa Catalina, over thirty miles distant.

As one would expect of a retreat center run by brothers imbued with the charism of Saint Francis, there are quiet trails and stations of the cross on the grounds that lead past pink geraniums, purple bougainvillea, orange poppies, and myriad other flowers. There are also secluded areas throughout, where it is possible to bask in peaceful solitude and enjoy life's simple pleasures: the warmth of the sun, the fragrance of the flowers, the lilting sounds of birdsong on the warm breeze.

top: Many rooms overlook the carefully tended gardens where guests easily find their own secluded corner.

bottom: Stairs lead to the newly built chapel. In the background, the rugged hills that surround the retreat to the north.

91

Caught between Flagstaff's San Francisco Peaks and Phoenix's Sonoran Desert is the region known as Red Rock country. For centuries, the area supported a score of Native American tribes who cultivated crops in Oak Creek Canyon and worshiped among the graceful rock formations. For them, this was the home of Grandmother Spirit, and the land itself was considered to be sacred and healing. Today, in the heart of the Red Rock country, Sedona continues that ancient tradition.

Once an isolated village and cattlemen's supply stop, and later, a retirement village and artists' colony, Sedona has recently become a mecca for visitors seeking alternative forms of therapy and worship. This sudden rise in popularity has changed and commercialized its peaceful ambience completely, but carved out of the side of Wilson Canyon, not far from the main town, John Paul Weber has fashioned with his own hands a healing and retreat facility that remains rustic and peaceful.

Healing Center of Arizona

25 Wilson Canyon Road

Sedona, Arizona 86336

602/282-7710

The setting for the Healing Center of Arizona, once a sacred Sinagua Indian site, is inspiring and just a little magical. Piñon, scrub oak, weathered juniper, and Arizona cypress carpet the canyon, filling the air with the pungent smell of pine resin. Across the canyon, stark red-brown cliffs rise above the forest, highlighted

That blessed mood

In which the burthen

of the mystery,

In which the heavy and

the weary weight

Of all this unintelligible world

Is lightened.

—William Wordsworth

by the backdrop of a crystalline turquoise sky. As the sun sets, the rocks seem to soften and reveal a shifting blend of pink, ocher, and rust, until their craggy outline disappears completely into the anthracite darkness of the Sedona night.

Weber, raised in Sedona, had established a healing center in San Francisco, the city where he had received degrees in nursing and psychology. In 1979, he returned to his hometown and bought a three-acre property to establish a healing center there. "Sedona amplifies," he says. "It tends to intensify everything. People are opened up to alternatives; work on yourself goes faster. Your dreams are louder." Weber, who had no prior construction experience, explains that he built the five-domed retreat center using mostly recycled materials and following instructions he received in his sleep from his five guides, including Jesus and Buddha. Weber spent the next nine years completing his dream with the help of friends and supporters.

Today, groups and individuals, both local and international, come to the Healing Center of Arizona for seminars, retreats, workshops, and plain old-fashioned relaxation. Couples on honeymoons, women's groups studying empowerment, rebirthers from Japan, psychiatrists from Phoenix, and businessmen from Britain have all taken advantage of the intimate setting that Weber has constructed. "It's like taking people into my home," he says. "They all become family."

A series of paths takes guests through the many levels of the Healing Center. Stops along the way include an outdoor hot tub with a view of the mountains, twenty raised flower and vegetable beds, including a rainbow-hued rose garden, and a quiet wooden *palapa*, where some of the friendly cats may want to share the hammock. A heart-shaped basketball court, also used for fire walks and sweat lodges, "is the only flat place around," says Weber. "It took three months to dig it out of the side of the hill." A swimming hole with icy cold water is a five-minute walk down the hillside to the creek below.

Up to thirty-five people can stay overnight at the Healing Center. The dormitory/meditation hall can sleep twenty, there are three sunny rooms, each with a queen-sized bed, and a geodesic dome among the trees, heated by a wood stove, can sleep several more.

Weber provides three gourmet vegetarian meals a day in the dining room that also doubles as a central meeting area. His choice of dishes is drawn from a wide range of cuisines, from Tibetan to Mexican, and the cost of meals is reasonable. Rates for overnight stays in the dormitory and tree house are well within the range of those on a budget. The private rooms are moderately priced—a bargain when compared with lodgings of comparable charm in the Sedona area.

"Most people who come here are looking to make changes," says Weber, but everyone is welcome to stay. "There are no expectations here." Practitioners of massage and many forms of alternative healing are familiar with the Healing Center, and can be called in for sessions. Perhaps the greatest compliment paid Weber is the fact that locals from Sedona often choose his Healing Center when they want a few days of peace and quiet from the invasion of tourists.

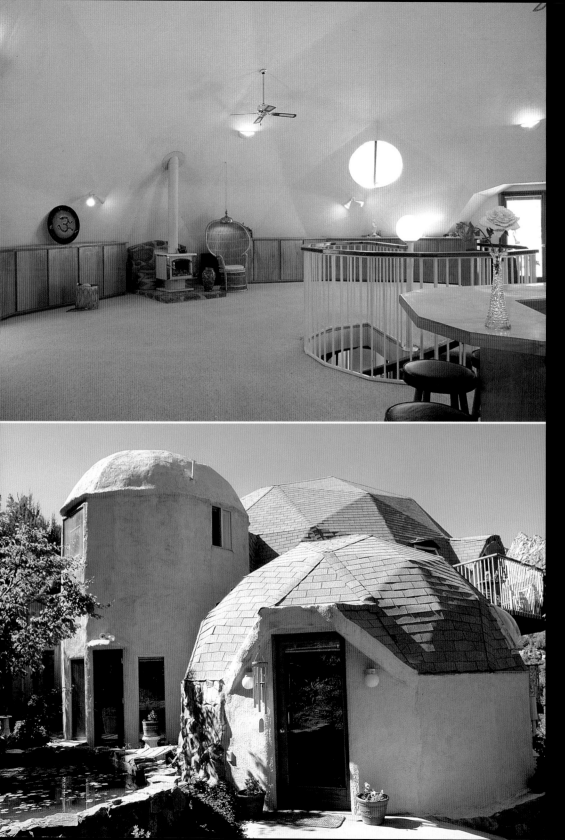

top: The main reception area also serves as a meeting room.

bottom: Five domes, clustered together like a bunch of daisies, were built by John Paul Weber with the help of his five "guides."

At first glance, Arcosanti looks like a mirage. Odd periscopic towers, strange winged apses, curved biomorphic mounds, and green spearlike cypresses rise abruptly from the barren mesa. The assemblage of trees and architecture looks for all the world as if it had fallen out of the sky, dropped by some passing mother ship from another galaxy.

Closer up, the sounds of Arcosanti are both worldly and ethereal: the rush of the desert wind, the chirping of birds, the occasional shriek of a peacock, and everywhere, the windbells—dry ceramic tones and deeper metallic sounds fill the shimmering air with their stochastic ringing.

These futuristic buildings reveal a past: there are signs everywhere that the desert wind and fierce Arizona sun has taken its toll on the structures. Most of these buildings are, in fact, almost a quarter of a century old. The site is called "Old Town" and consists of residences, bronze and ceramics studios, a gallery, a bakery, a cafe, offices, conference and lecture rooms, studios, workshops, and an amphitheater.

Arcosanti is the vision of architect Paolo Soleri, and Old Town represents only four percent of what he had planned for these basalt cliffs overlooking the Agua Fria River. Soleri's original vision for this bleak mesa was the construction of a thriving city of five thousand,

Arcosanti

HC 74 Box 4136

Mayer, Arizona 86333

602/632-7135

If the sacred is where life is, then
the whole habitat is sacred.
—Paolo Soleri

covering fifteen acres, with arresting structures twenty-five stories high that would change forever the way cities were built.

Born in Italy, Soleri came to the Arizona desert in 1947 to work with Frank Lloyd Wright. Over the next two decades, he developed his concept of "arcology" (the word is a contraction of *architecture* and *ecology*), by which he meant a "methodology that recognizes the necessity of the radical reorganization of the sprawling urban landscape into dense integrated three-dimensional cities." Arcosanti (a contraction of *arcology* and the Italian words *cosa* and *anti*, meaning "before" or "without things") was to be the prototype of just such a city. In 1969, Soleri bought 860 acres and leased 3,200 more from the state in the high desert seventy miles north of Phoenix.

Construction began in 1970. It was a heady time, the end of a decade of upheaval and ferment, and while some revolutionaries were tearing down institutions, in 1970, Soleri and his enthusiastic supporters set about constructing one in the Arizona desert. Enthusiasm was high as volunteers from around the world arrived to realize Soleri's dream. But as years, then decades, passed, fewer volunteers showed up, and lack of funding stalled the project at the present Old Town phase. Soleri's new timetable calls for the completion of a "Critical Mass" phase, with five hundred Arcosantians continuing his vision of arcology into the twenty-first century.

Over four thousand volunteers have helped build Arcosanti over the years. Currently, some sixty people live at Arcosanti, although the number varies seasonally. Whether craftspeople, cooks, engineers, or carpenters, they share the common belief that Arcosanti is, above all, a necessary project for the world—a demonstration that there is an alternative to the land-devouring megalopolis and its rampant materialism.

Forty thousand people a year enjoy day visits to Arcosanti and see this vision in practice. Entrance fees are modest, and meals and baked goods are home-cooked and reasonably priced. Many of these visitors purchase the distinctive windbells that seem to hang everywhere at Arcosanti. In a process devised by Soleri, silt, an earthy sediment of clay and sand found naturally in riverbeds, is carved to create the bells' original shapes. The bronze is poured into negative sand molds in Arcosanti's own foundry. Some bells are finished to a golden, burnished luster while others are dipped in muriatic acid, leaving unique patterns of turquoise and pastel and earth tones on the surface, similar to the colors of the sand, sky, and mountains of the desert surrounding Arcosanti. The ceramic bells, fashioned from Arizona clay, are also formed and fired at Arcosanti. Soleri windbells, now sold in galleries and shipped around the world, provide Arcosanti with the bulk of its income.

Popular weeklong workshops in silt carving and casting, including special sessions for children, are held monthly. One-week academic seminars, also held monthly, offer an introduction to Arcosanti and include a question-and-answer session with Soleri. Participants in the introductory seminar are eligible to join in a four-week hands-on construction workshop, helping to build and maintain Arcosanti. Those interested in alternative agriculture enjoy working in the

previous page: Italian cypresses overlook basalt cliffs at the edge of the Old Town section of Arcosanti.

left: Handcast windbells of all sizes are found in every building. Their sale helps support Arcosanti, the vision of Paolo Soleri.

small organic vegetable and herb garden, an experimental greenhouse, and the peach orchard.

Those attending workshops stay in a lower campground equipped with electricity, toilets, showers, and simple living shelters. Vans and tents can sometimes be accommodated at the campsite. Workshop fees are reasonable and cover tuition, room, and three meals a day of wholesome food at the cafe.

There are also limited overnight accommodations at modest rates for up to a dozen guests in very simple single and double rooms, some with shared bathrooms. There is no air conditioning to temper the 100-plus-degree temperatures in summer and no central heating to warm the winter nights when temperatures can drop below freezing. A twenty-five-meter swimming pool is open during the warm months.

A lone two-bedroom Sky Suite, with its own kitchen, is reasonably priced, has a superb view of the desert, and offers the opportunity to live in a Soleri-designed environment. In keeping with the ethos of Arcosanti, that environment is compact, spare, and functional, a testament to the emphasis Soleri places on the dynamic relationships between people, not on material objects. Arcosanti may look as if it were dropped from outer space, but the impulse behind it is purely humanist.

A view of one of the main buildings in the Old Town section, with a commanding view of the endless Arizona desert.

There are many deserts, some bleak and barren, but the desert surrounding the Picture Rocks Retreat and the Desert House of Prayer teems with life. In spring, the pale green paloverde trees stand brimming with clusters of yellow flowers, and even the ancient saguaro cacti sport crowns of frail white flowers. Hummingbirds zoom among the blossoms while jackrabbits watch curiously before disappearing leisurely behind the grey-ball sage. This is not a desert that challenges the visitor with a feeling of exposure and emptiness. There is, to be sure, an overwhelming feeling of openness and freedom in these expanses, but the hardy environment paradoxically seems also to embrace and protect.

Picture Rocks Retreat

7101 W. Picture Rocks Road

Tucson, Arizona 85743

602/744-3400

Desert House of Prayer

7350 W. Picture Rocks Road,

Tucson, Arizona 85743

602/744-3825

(mailing address)

P.O. Box 574

Cortaro, Arizona 85652

The external environment is mirrored in the openness and nurturing of the dedicated staff of Redemptorist Women and Lay Volunteers who run both the Retreat and the House of Prayer. The Redemptorists were founded in 1732 when the young priest Alphonsus Ligouri gathered a small band of priests in Naples to preach to the poor and the abandoned in the rural districts. The staff at Picture Rocks continues that tradition in a setting where the silence of the desert can carry the strongest message for those seeking inner peace. "Silence does speak loudly here," says one sister. "We're not hemmed in by a lot of people."

I will lead you into the desert, and

there I will speak to your heart.

—Hosea 2:14

The land itself has always been sacred. The Hohokam Native American tribe passed through this land on hunting expeditions, leaving petroglyphs now some 1,500 years old that endure to this day. Chipped on the western face of a mound of rocks a short walk from the chapel are images of hunters, spirals, zoomorphic forms, and headdressed dancing figures.

Nothing had ever been built on this holy ground until 1963, when the bishop of Tucson invited the Oakland-based order to found a retreat center in the desert. Today, Picture Rocks offers a range of one-day seminars on spirituality and a variety of subjects. Longer retreats, including weekends, are also offered. Guests arriving for individual retreats are also welcome and may receive spiritual guidance, if desired.

Up to eighty people can be accommodated at Picture Rocks in double and single rooms, all of which come equipped with heating and air-conditioning. Rates for seminars are modest, and weekend retreats, including meals, are reasonably priced. The food, which includes meat but can be made vegetarian with prior notice, is well balanced and nourishing, and a well-stocked salad bar accompanies lunches and dinners. Meals are served cafeteria-style in the dining room that overlooks the lights of the northeastern edge of Tucson—a reminder of how removed this quiet retreat center is from the cares and concerns of the workaday world.

previous page: A giant saguaro cactus stands guard over a verdant desert and the low mound of stones known as "the picture rocks."

left: A bell in the desert calls the guests at the Desert House of Prayer to worship.

The Desert House of Prayer, across the road, is a smaller, more intimate setting designed for those seeking a more inward, contemplative experience. The word *House* is figurative; there is a small complex of buildings, including a chapel, library, and dining area, but the reference, according to Father John Kane, the retreat's founder, is "not so much to a building as it is to a group of people who come together for the search for quiet and that inner reality."

The staff of six pray twice daily, mornings and evenings, preceding the liturgy with an hour of quiet seated meditation, broken by a short period of walking meditation, a technique akin to that practiced in Soto Zen. "That's our communion. We go into the darkness and touch the God present within us."

The atmosphere at the Desert House is relaxed and there are no requirements beyond respecting the silence and needs of other retreatants. Many guests may choose to work for an hour or so each day, helping in the kitchen or doing simple housekeeping or groundskeeping chores. Some guests make good use of the easygoing contemplative setting and sleep, rest, and recuperate from their often highly active lives. Many of these are caregivers who minister to others and arrive at Desert House "tired, suffering from burnout or overwork, dead emotionally," says Father John. "We consider it a privilege to help them." But guests at Desert House come from all walks of life. One author stayed in a hermitage for seven months while working on her autobiography.

Those thinking of staying at Desert House are advised to make an initial visit of one or two days to determine if they feel comfortable with the setting and the silence. A minimum stay of one week is recommended to allow the "inner transformation"—the healing and centering—to take place. Up to nine guests can stay in simple rooms, each equipped with an evaporative cooler. There are also three separate hermitages.

Healthy, substantial food is prepared by the staff in their own kitchen. Guests serve themselves at breakfast and lunch. Both these meals are eaten in silence, but breakfast is rarely a quiet affair. Scores of birds of many species—including brilliantly plumed tanagers, orioles, and cardinals—swoop down on the bird feeders each morning, chirping, fluttering, and twittering in what has come to be a high point of the day for many guests. Dinners are sit-down and served. They are congenial gatherings where the staff and the guests can share their thoughts and joys.

After dinner, guests may linger in the well-stocked library, return to their rooms, or take a long contemplative walk in the desert. As the sun sets, the sky turns into a wash of ever deepening pinks, outlining the sharp edges of the distant mountains and the almost human forms of the giant saguaro cacti. This desert is indeed mysterious, calming, and healing.

top: The airy chapel was built virtually single-handedly by an Irish stonemason.

bottom: The petroglyphs, estimated to be some 1,500 years old, were left by passing members of the Hohokam tribe.

Paloverde trees and prickly pear cacti blossom in the vibrant desert above Tucson.

Benet Pines Retreat Center is an intimate community and retreat center on the top of a watershed in the high country of Colorado (altitude 7,000 feet). Three members of the Benet Hill Benedictine Sisters of Colorado Springs live here, providing a prayerful, hospitable environment "where all who come can discover more fully their God, and themselves."

Community is central to the Benet Hill experience. "Guests are invited to share in our prayers and share in our meals." These sisters enjoy the peaceful natural setting, yet they are also activists: many in their order teach, work in hospitals, or are engaged in parish work. "What's unique here is our struggle between the active and the contemplative prayer life," says one sister. "There is a stress to create a rhythm and a balance, but it's a stress that a layperson can identify with."

The thirty-three-acre setting of dense pine forest will certainly help anyone seeking peace and quiet to find their own personal balance. From the main house looking west, the pine trees frame the imposing profile of Pikes Peak, whose granite-topped summit was said to inspire Katharine Lee Bates to write "America the Beautiful." In the spring, each breath is filled with the odor of pine and resin, and golden columbine, purple penstemon, wild roses, and delicate paint brush flower among the trees. In the winter, the boughs are shagged with snow, and the deep cushion of pine needles on the forest floor

Benet Pines Retreat Center

15780 Highway 83

Colorado Springs, Colorado 80921

719/495-2574

Midwinter late sun flashes

through hilltops and trees

a good day . . .

—Gary Snyder

muffles all but the faintest sounds of footfall. In this setting of trees and wind, the silence is a peaceful backdrop for contemplation and divining one's innermost thoughts.

Benet Pines can host up to seventeen guests in a homey, completely noninstitutional atmosphere. The larger house has four bedrooms, a kitchen, and a large meeting room in the basement. A smaller house has four bedrooms and a kitchen. Two hermitages are simple and rustic, lacking even running water; a third is a completely self-contained unit. Guests can either cook for themselves or join the sisters for a cuisine that is mostly, but not exclusively, vegetarian.

previous page: The pine forest at Benet Pines is dense. The mountain air, pure and clear.

left: One of the two main guest houses set among the trees.

Winters are generally mild, and the altitude tempers the summer heat, but nights year-round are chilly. Colorado Springs is half an hour away, and there are miles of hiking trails in the area, but when it rains, the roads and exposed ground turn into heavy mud. At night, the sky is a dark velvet dome awash with stars and the sparkling swath of the Milky Way.

"Our doors are open to any seeker," says one sister, "if they respect nature and each other." Guests are welcome to phone, then drop by for a day. If they choose, they may also stay overnight or for up to a month at a time.

Suggested donations, which include meals, are reasonable, and sabbaticals (work exchanges) are available for longer stays. The staff prays three times a day, at 8:00 A.M., noon, and 5:30 P.M., and guests are invited to join. However, no requirements are placed on visitors, save for the injunction by the friendly sisters at Benet Pines "to let your spirit and your body rest."

The community invites guests "to come and discover more fully their God, and themselves." The forest (top) and modest accommodations (bottom) provide the setting for that quest.

In the twelfth century, a dedicated group of Carmelite monks led a simple and austere life of contemplation on the holy mount that was to provide their name. Today, in Colorado, at the foot of another Mount Carmel, a small group of men and women have returned to that primitive Carmelite spirit in a monastery that melds the medieval and the modern.

The chapel and buildings of Nada Hermitage rise out of the rabbit brush and sand at the edge of the high, flat desert. To the south, the San Luis Valley extends to the New Mexico border and beyond—some seventy-five miles in clear weather. To the east, the high rocky peaks of the Sangre de Cristo Mountains, including Mount Carmel (marked on the maps as Kit Carson Peak) soar over fouteen thousand feet and dominate the vista. The sky here is ever changing, a welter of weather systems, clouds, shifting winds, and startling flashes of sunlight made sharp and hard by the clean, thin air.

Jon Worden, the architect for the Sangre de Cristo Chapel, dedicated in 1985, set the tone for the rest of the monastery, including the final eight hermitages completed in 1991. Like the community itself, the structures at Nada are earthy but not earthbound. In the rhythm of the rooflines, the buildings reflect the silhouette of the mountains.

Nada Hermitage, Spiritual Life Institute

P.O. Box 219

Crestone, Colorado 81131

719/256-4778

We need the tonic of wilderness . . .

—Henry David Thoreau

The shape of the bell tower, buttresses, and turrets and almost haphazard placement of all the buildings are reminiscent of medieval monasteries. Yet, throughout, details such as adobe-like stucco, Ponderosa pine posts, and tile scuppers celebrate the building traditions of the Southwest. Modern technology is put to use, too. The buildings are dug well into the sand, protected from the elements, while the southern exposures are all glass, providing for passive solar heating so efficient that windows must be cracked opened on many a winter's day.

The Nada Hermitage is the outcome of a seminal dialogue in the late 1950s between Father William McNamara, the community's founder, and Thomas Merton. Together, they investigated the future shape of the contemplative life in the Western world. The original monastery in Sedona, Arizona, soon outgrew its nine-acre plot, and in 1982, the Spiritual Life Community moved to its present site on seventy acres of donated land near Crestone.

Today, nine monks and nuns live at Nada (a Spanish word meaning "nothing"). It is the wilderness, the barren desert environment, which sustains those who live here. "There's a strong sense of challenge in the desert," says one brother. "In the wilderness, we all open to a larger transcendent experience." In their separate hermitages, the members of this community follow the *Carmelite Rule of Saint Albert* and "meditate day and night on the law of the Lord unless engaged in some other just occupation." Other just occupations may include morning and evening sessions of prayer or activities as apparently mundane as chopping

wood or feeding donkeys. At Nada, all the day's activities are considered to be the foundation for a vital, spiritual life. "Our best religious activities are those where religion is least emphasized."

On Sunday, the community members "break their ordinary pattern of existence and waste the day by praying and playing." In the late morning, following mass, the community gathers in the dining room around the long pine table for lunch. There they share their thoughts—but only one person is permitted to speak at a time.

previous page: Rabbit brush and mountains frame the buildings at Nada. The architecture plays with the random placement and design elements of a medieval castle, monastery, and town.

left: The interior of a hermitage cabin. The stucco, exposed wood beams, and tiles celebrate the building traditions of the Southwest.

There are sixteen hermitages, so there is usually room for about six or seven guests who arrive for individual retreats and "the simplicity, the silence, and the closeness to nature." Guests share in the community's rhythms of solitude in their own hermitages, each of which bears the name of a religious leader, such as Gandhi, Cardinal Newman, or Dorothy Day (founder of the Catholic Worker Movement). The hermitages have electricity and are completely self-contained, including a kitchen and a small wood stove for heating. Piles of chopped wood outside the hermitage doors are a feature of the monastery. Inside, the hermitages are spare and comfortable, with exposed pine beams set against white stucco.

Each hermitage also comes with a basic supply of staples and grains. The pantry in the main building provides fresh organic vegetables, some of which are from the monastery's own walled garden, and large pots of homemade soup and rice, to be taken back to the individual hermitages and eaten in solitude.

In Agape, the main meeting area, there is an excellent library of books on all areas of contemplation and spirituality, works by authors such as Alan Watts, Thomas Merton, and Saint John of the Cross. There is also an ample collection of audio tapes, from operas to recorded sets of seminal religious conferences.

Suggested donations for retreats are moderate; couples may stay for a slight additional charge. Nada is open to people of all denominations, but accepted guests are requested to arrive only on Thursday afternoons and to depart on Wednesdays by noon. Manual labor with the monks is required on Saturday mornings and encouraged at other times. Guided tours are on Saturdays from noon to 1:00 P.M. only; no other tours will be permitted.

Nada is a warmhearted community in a severe and barren land. It is the kind of place that can, and will, change one's life. "What do I think of Nada?" one guest wrote. "Words impoverish. Unique, unforgettable, soul-stirring—none of these adjectives is adequate. My experience was at once tempestuous and calming, a wrestling and a dancing, a stillness and a cry. Here, no fakery is possible, no pseudolife. Here you face yourself, the earth, and God—naked (nada). Here you flame, or die."

top: The imposing Sangre de Cristo Mountains provide a rugged backdrop at Nada.

bottom: Hermitage cabins are fully self-contained, with kitchens and wood stoves. Piles of wood are found beside each cabin.

The simple stone altar and wood and bronze cross of Christ, sculpted by Dan Davidson of Santa Fe, are bracketed by stained glass windows. Designed by Mother Tessa Bielecki and fashioned by Denver artists, the window portrays a Native American, a Southea Asian refugee mother and child, and a black slave.

The faded Tibetan prayer flags that greet the visitor to the Lama Foundation serve a higher purpose than mere fluttering decoration. The frail cotton pennants are designed so that the mountain wind will unravel them and carry their messages of peace, thread by delicate thread, to the furthest reaches of the earth. The Lama Foundation, like the prayer flags made here, is a community with a similar mission—to bring peace and understanding to the world through prayer, teaching and sharing the truths and practices of many traditions.

Located on the northwestern edge of the Sangre de Cristo Mountains, the Lama Foundation covers a hundred acres of forest and meadows. Situated at a height of 8,600 feet, the air is always crystalline, redolent of piñon, pine, and mountain meadow in the summertime. The view is breathtaking. The low rounded peaks of the San Juan Mountains, fully eighty miles distant, mark the edge of the western horizon, beyond the expanse of the Cebolla Mesa and the dark line creasing it that is the Rio Grande Gorge.

Lama was incorporated in 1967 as an "instrument for the awakening and evolution of consciousness" and came to national recognition as the location where Ram Dass wrote *Be Here Now*, the

Lama Foundation

P.O. Box 240

San Cristobal, New Mexico 87564

505/586-1269

Our abiding teacher is the
mountain itself, with its silence
and ancient, undisturbed peace.
—Lama Foundation

well-known introduction to spirituality and consciousness raising. The architecture, reflecting the mixing of East and West found in that book, is a unique amalgam of the ancient and modern. Some of the main dwelling houses and meditation halls resemble kivas; others are thoroughly modern geodesic domes. Many buildings meld adobe and glass together seamlessly, and throughout, there are motifs reminiscent of dwellings found in the Himalayas. The central meditation hall, built in 1970, is fashioned in the tradition of a Native American prayer chamber, or kiva, and received the blessing of the local elders.

The foundation's land contains one of the few natural springs in the area—its source of water—and sits astride the Kiowa Peace Trail, a historic trading artery from north to south used by many tribes for peaceful passage. The respect for the peaceful and ancient ways of those who passed through this land continues. "Almost every spot on the land has been infused with prayer," says one Lama community member. And in a concrete example of swords to plowshares, the gongs that call visitors to meals and meditation are fashioned from the nose cones of Cold War missiles.

Community is central to the Lama experience. "We're not a retreat center," notes one foundation member. "We're a community that offers retreats." Most community members are in their midtwenties,

and their youthful enthusiasm is palpable and infectious, helping to balance the deep seriousness of the spiritual enterprise with a continual leavening of play.

Lama offers a variety of self-contained workshops each summer in a range of traditions, from Sufism and Christian Mysticism to yogic practices and Hasidism. Activities for participants may range from vision quests to Sufi Dances of Universal Peace to a Japanese tea ceremony. Those interested in the Lama community will benefit from the annual introductory orientation seminar. The foundation also provides isolated hermitages for extended private retreats.

previous page: The interior of a large geodesic dome, used as one of the main meeting areas.

left: The accommodations are simple, in keeping with the desire to pare down to essentials.

Overnight visitors are expected to participate in shared work (known as "karma yoga") for a few hours each day. Most choose to help in the kitchen, but if you have needed skills, your efforts will be appreciated elsewhere. A workshop on the site, for instance, produces the prayer flags fluttering throughout their land.

Lama is open to outsiders only during the summer months. Several specific Sundays are set aside for day visits, and other ways of visiting Lama may vary from summer to summer. (Please call ahead to arrange visits.)

Accommodations are basic and as eclectic as the workshops, ranging from the graceful and peace-inspiring main adobe and wood structures to tepees and dormitory cabins. Most visitors stay in their own tents. A separate self-contained retreat center can serve groups of up to twenty-five.

The simple but nutritious vegetarian fare is eaten communally, either in the dining room perched atop the kitchen or in the adjacent grassy areas when the weather permits.

The Lama Foundation gets its name from the Spanish word for "mud." The name is apt, especially after a heavy rain; bring your boots. The road that climbs the mountain, especially for the last two miles, can become sodden and slippery after wet weather, but the difficult ascent is rewarded by the sight of windblown prayer flags and the friendly smiles of this community of seekers for whom this mountaintop is a sacred home.

top: The prayer flags flutter in front of one of the meditation and meeting structures. Handmade onsite (below) the prayer flags are distributed throughout the world, carrying their messages of peace to all nations.

The stark setting at Ghost Ranch inspires, even demands, a sense of wonder. Razor-thin mesas rise from the dusty plain, a flotilla of chalky ships on a sere sea of ocher and brown. Closer in, red fingers of wind-worn rock and ragged cliffs of sandstone jut into the turquoise sky.

The setting is rugged, but the environment is fragile: rainfall rarely exceeds ten inches per year. The residents and supporters of the Ghost Ranch are well aware of that fact and value their role as the stewards of this unique part of the world. They instill a deep respect for the ecology here through classes and use innovative land-management techniques to husband and develop the resources on these twenty-one thousand acres of high mountain desert.

Two hundred fifty million years ago, the dry ground was once covered with tropical swamps, mimosa trees, and broad expanses of horsetail grass. Digs carried out on the ranch have revealed a wealth of dinosaur bones from those times, including fossils of the earliest known dinosaur, coelophysis. As a result, the Ghost Ranch is now a Registered Natural Landmark and houses its own paleontology museum. There is also an abundance of Native American artifacts scattered throughout the land, left through the millennia by those who lived and hunted in these cañons and mesas.

Ghost Ranch Conference Center

HC 77 Box 11

Abiquiu, New Mexico 87510-9601

505/685-4333

By all means use sometimes to
be alone.
Salute thyself: see what thy soul
doth wear
—George Herbert

The ranch itself was first ceded by the king of Spain in the late eighteenth century and became known as *El Rancho de los Brujos*—Ranch of the Sorcerers, a place haunted by powerful spirits. Tales of ghostly wailing babies, a giant snake, a flying red cow, and a murderous brother added to the mystique. After passing through a succession of owners, the land was purchased by Arthur and Phoebe Pack in 1933, who turned it into a dude ranch. In 1955, the Packs gave the land to the Presbyterian Church, and in 1972, a foundation was established to support the ministry of the Ghost Ranch and its operations as a national adult study and conference center. Local residents now agree that the Ghost Ranch, once possessed by evil spirits, is now inhabited by a spirit of a very different sort, one grounded in a respect for the earth and a faith in the future.

previous page: Chimney rock, carved by millennia of wind and water, is only one of the many striking features of the landscape in this area.

left: The setting at Ghost Ranch is a favorite of film makers. This cabin was built for the movie *City Slickers*. In the background (below) is Pedernal, the ancient volcano that artist Georgia O'Keeffe admired and often painted.

Georgia O'Keeffe, who immortalized the arresting landscape through her painting, lived for a time on a small parcel of land near the ranch property, although the artist was not involved with the ranch activities. Pedernal, the flat-topped mountain to the south, was perhaps her favorite subject. "It's my private mountain," she frequently said. "God told me if I painted it often enough I could have it." O'Keeffe's now famous drawing of a bleached steer skull was adopted as the ranch's logo in 1971. The image hearkens to the time when, in the 1930s, the narrow dirt road leading up Chama River Valley to the Ghost Ranch was marked by a single animal skull propped against a rock.

Today, the road to the Ghost Ranch from Abiquiu is far easier to find, and each year, thousands follow it. Many nonprofit, civic, arts, and other groups choose the Ghost Ranch as the site of their annual meetings. There are also countless individuals who arrive each year to take advantage of the wealth of artistic, self-improvement, and educational courses and workshops offered.

"People have to learn to make choices here," said one resident. "There is so much going on." The choices are eclectic, ranging from courses on poetry composition, ceramics, or wilderness photography to sessions with titles such as "Ecology, Geology and the Cosmos." About a dozen Elderhostels are held in the fall and spring.

Many families and clans also use the Ghost Ranch as a gathering place where children and grandchildren scattered in cities across the continent can return each year to reunite. For them, as for the hundreds who return each year for a pilgrimage of rest and relaxation, Ghost Ranch is considered a true second home.

The fees overall are reasonable, especially for the campsites, and the course and class costs are well within any budget. Service arrangements, whereby visitors work for a few hours each day on the ranch, can reduce the cost of a stay here even further.

Given all the courses and groups meeting at any one time, the Ghost Ranch can feel akin to a college campus, albeit set in the wilds of

New Mexico. There are several lounges, a cafeteria that can serve 1,200 vegetarian and nonvegetarian meals a day, an extensive library open twenty-four hours, three museums, and even an adjacent high desert research farm. A variety of meeting rooms is available for groups of all sizes, and a total of 350 people can be accommodated in a variety of dwellings, from adobe houses and simple motel-style double rooms to Spartan wooden dormitories and a range of campsites.

The main compound of the Ghost Ranch fairly bustles with activity year-round as groups and families arrive, meet, mingle, and depart on a daily basis. Yet, despite the wealth of enticing activities, the option of undisturbed solitude is only minutes away and remains the Ghost Ranch's strongest attraction.

Follow any of the narrow footpaths away from the main cluster of buildings and the visitor can walk directly into a harsh and quiet land, where the pervasive silence is broken by the sound of the winds carving their way through the piñons and the juniper bushes. Covering an area of almost forty square miles, trails on the Ghost Ranch lead for miles in all directions. Once in the wilderness on the mesa, it is possible to wander for days through this timeless land and never meet another soul. It is with good reason that one of the many courses offered at Ghost Ranch is "Desert Wisdom and Contemplative Prayer."

top and bottom: A delicate environment in a rugged land. Strata on the exposed sides of the mesas reveal their geological history. Millions of years ago this high desert area was once a swamp.

The Monastery of Christ in the Desert is hidden at the end of a thirteen-mile dirt road in the rugged beauty of Chama Canyon. From afar, the only sign of its existence is the award-winning chapel, designed by Japanese architect George Nakashima, which rises with clean modern lines from the ancient soil. From within that brick and stone structure, a broad wall of glass above the altar reveals a stunning view of steep crags—the shattered red cliffs that shelter the monastery to the east.

The sheer magnificence of the setting inspires a mixture of awe and humility. Thomas Merton stayed here and loved it. "I have been summoned," he wrote, "to explore a desert area of man's heart in which explanations no longer suffice. An arid, rocky, dark land of the soul, sometimes illuminated by strange fires." Like the Benedictine monks who live here year-round, Merton found the stark setting a fertile one for his life of introspection.

Monastery of Christ in the Desert

Abiquiu, New Mexico 87510

Visitors on individual retreats and those who wish a respite from the urban pace of life will find the setting, and the isolation, equally as fertile. They must, however, be prepared for life in the New Mexican high desert. Winters can be downright chilly and snow may fall; summers are merciless. In the hottest months, temperatures easily pass the 100-degree mark, but even on the most withering days, the furnacelike conditions are tempered by the nearby Chama River and its calming

O God of truth, . . . You send the

beauty of the dawn,

And the burning heat of noon.

—Saint Ambrose

susurrus of rushing water. Thanks to this flow, there is always the presence of green along its banks and throughout the fields of the monastery.

The monastery was founded in 1964 by Father Aelred Wall, OSB, and two monks from a monastery in New York. A community of some twenty Benedictine monks drawn from many countries lives on the 275-acre site, with another eight monks at an associated monastery in central Mexico.

The community strictly follows the Rule of their founder, Saint Benedict. All the monks have taken the vow of stability, a lifelong commitment to the monastery, and fulfill the dictum of *ora et labora*—prayer and work. Community members rise before dawn to greet the day in the dark canyon with prayer and Gregorian chants.

The Rule of Saint Benedict includes the welcome reception of guests. Visitors to the monastery are encouraged, as one community member explained, "to share the life of the monks as much as they feel comfortable." That may include worship, or work, or both. Visitors may help out with groundskeeping, housekeeping, or, should they possess the skills, tasks that are often in need of completion in isolated locations, such as repairing vehicles or attending to the solar power supply system.

Meals are taken communally, buffet-style, and the food prepared by the monks is tasty, nourishing, and unadorned, in keeping with the simplicity of the life here. Classical music may accompany some meals; at others, a community member reads from the Scriptures and a selection of books on religious themes, such as biographies of popes or well-known theologians.

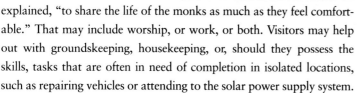

Accommodations are as basic as the food: nine simple rooms with *banco* (raised adobe brick) beds in the adobe visitor's complex. Each of the rooms opens onto a courtyard covered in gravel punctuated by the occasional cactus, small beds of hardy flowers, and a sunbaked wooden sculpture of Saint Francis. There is running water but no electricity in the rooms; kerosene lamps are provided for lighting.

There is a gift shop, a common room, and a lounge with a small kitchenette where guests can relax together. The reading room, adjacent to the refectory, is designed for study, and the library is well stocked with both religious and secular titles. One is as likely to find works by James Joyce as a tome on the lives of the saints.

previous page: The striking glass and stone chapel, designed by George Nakashima, confronts the rugged setting of Chama Canyon.

top: The refectory is reached by way of the well-stocked library.

bottom: The smoke of incense rises above the simple stone altar inside the chapel.

It is possible to make a day visit to this desert setting, but two days is the recommended minimum length of stay to forget the pace of the city and enter fully into the rhythm of the monastery. A sleeping bag is needed in the wintertime, when it can snow. Hats, loose clothing, and sunblock are recommended in the summer.

The road to the monastery (Forest Service Road 151) is a single-lane track, solid and hard-packed, with little washboarding. All vehicles can negotiate it when dry. When it rains or snows, however, the road can become slippery and dangerous. Visitors without a four-wheel-drive vehicle should wait until the road surface dries enough to provide adequate traction.

Day visitors are welcome to the monastery, but those who wish to stay overnight must first contact the guest master by mail.

top: A sculpture of St. Francis faces the guests' quarters, with the cliffs of Chama Canyon in the background.

bottom: Wooden seats in the chapel for community members. The brothers rise before dawn to greet their day with prayer and chants.

The Pecos Benedictine Monastery stands at the edge of a wilderness, on the upper reaches of the Pecos River. An aromatic mix of piñon, juniper, Ponderosa pine, and Douglas fir extends north as far the eye can see into the high spruce forests of the Pecos Wilderness Area. Rising to the west are the tree-covered foothills of the Sangre de Cristo Mountains and, beyond, the rocky summits of the Truchas Peaks. At thirteen thousand feet, these rugged mountains keep their occasional winter dusting of snow long after it has melted away in the valley far below.

The setting is enchanting, and in the Land of Enchantment, it is only fitting that the monastic community at Pecos is guided by dreams and by visions. "We're a charismatic community," says one brother. "The gifts of the Spirit are at work here."

Pecos, a former Spanish land grant and working ranch, has a long history as a retreat center: the first *cursillo* (little course in Christianity) in the United States was held here. In 1908, it became a dude ranch that Trappists took over following World War II. They were unable to survive as a community of subsistence farmers and sold the property in 1955 to the Benedictines of Benet Lake, Wisconsin, who retained the title given it by the Trappists—Our Lady of Guadalupe Monastery.

Pecos Benedictine Monastery

Pecos, New Mexico 87552

505/757-6415

128

Your old men shall dream
dreams, your young men shall
see visions.
—Joel 2:28

In 1969, the charismatic element came to Pecos in the person of Father (later, Abbot) David Geraets. He was following a dream that he interpreted as his guiding purpose in life: to establish centers of Pentecostal spirituality throughout the nation. He and three other brothers came to Pecos from Wisconsin to make that dream a reality. In barely a quarter of a century, Pecos has become the largest of a growing network of monasteries where personal mystical experiences—the charismata of praying and preaching in tongues, spiritual and physical healing, and prophetic revelations in dreams and visions—are nurtured and accepted.

In 1970, the monastery took a progressive step when it accepted women into its midst. "Each of us is both masculine and feminine," says one brother. "In a double community, we make that a living statement. It's a restoration of balance." The move to include women, however, was not recognized by the congregation to which Pecos then belonged, and it was not until 1985 that the "double monastery" was officially sanctioned, following the community's adoption by the Olivetan Congregation of Benedictines. Today, women are integral partners with men at the monastery.

The community prays together four times a day in the low, modest chapel in the main building. Sometimes an organ or the quiet strumming of a guitar accompanies the prayers. After compline, or night prayers, members of the community may stay in the chapel,

previous page: "There is a felt experience of peace at Pecos," says one brother. The monastery is located on the banks of the Pecos River, which continues through New Mexico to Texas, where it flows into the Rio Grande.

left: There are many areas throughout the monastery's grounds for quiet walks or gentle conversation.

uttering unknown languages, singing ethereal melodies, whispering and praying as they experience the ineffable gifts of the Spirit.

Depth psychology—especially some of the writings of Carl Jung—is also part of the fabric of religious life at Pecos. "Some of his insights mesh beautifully with Christianity," says one brother. "Especially his writings on dreams."

Pecos hosts weekend retreats, where up to sixty-five participants from all denominations gather to learn the many sources and approaches to what is known at Pecos as "wholistic spirituality." Study sessions, for instance, may focus on the enneagram as well as biblical exegesis. Diet, exercise, and movement are also stressed; one retreat is "Encountering the Lord of the Dance."

Many of these retreats are directed toward curing the "pathology of the soul": reappraising relationships, coping with midlife crises, dealing with recovering alcoholism, and overcoming the trauma of childhood abuse. "I have seen many inner healings here," says one monk. "And some startling physical healings, too."

While the outdoor setting for this inner healing is spectacular, the interior of the monastery building itself, despite its attractive adobe exterior, is more mundane. "It's your basic Motel 6," says one brother from the wing with plain rooms that can house up to sixty-five people in shared accommodations. Three healthful meals, nonvegetarian but with little red meat, are served family-style and eaten with community members at round wooden tables in the upstairs refectory.

Individuals can come for private retreats at Pecos between Mondays and Fridays, with or without spiritual direction. Midweek guests are free to follow their own agenda, but they are encouraged to be at prayers and Eucharist. Suggested donations at Pecos for program and individual retreats, which include all meals, are extremely reasonable.

There is a well-stocked bookstore, where volumes on the Bible sit beside books by Robert Bly, Alice Miller, and, of course, Carl Jung. The monastery also operates Dove Publications, a thriving mail-order book sales operation with a broad range of offerings on inner healing, including several series of audio cassettes on depth psychology.

For many who visit this pioneering monastery, the greatest healing may take place in solitude while standing on the bank of the Pecos River surrounded by wild irises, lupine, and purple penstemon. "There is a felt experience of peace at Pecos," explains one brother. "Monks have been here since 1947, and those prayers tend to penetrate the buildings and the property."

The buildings' design replicates the classic adobe features of the Southwest.